The Panama Papers

The Largest Financial Scandal of Modern Times

Volume 1

By Simon Luria

Contents

The Panama Papers ....
Copyright information ....
Source Material and Disclaimer ....
Preface ....
Introduction ....
The Shell Game ....
Mossack Fonseca: The Registered Agent of Record ....
Hidden In the Shadows ....
Mossack Fonseca - The Response ....
The Oracle of Brooklyn? ....
Are Rumors Just Unconfirmed Facts? ....
The Fonseca Fallout ....
Final Thoughts ....
Recommended Reading ....
Upcoming Books by the Author ....
Source Material ....

Copyright information

Copyright © 2016 by Simon Luria

All rights reserved. No part of this book may be reproduced by any mechanical, photographic, or electrical process, or in the form of a recording. Nor may it be stored in a storage/retrieval system nor transmitted or otherwise be copied for private or public use-other than "fair use" as quotations in articles or reviews—without the prior written consent of the Author.

The Information in this book is solely for educational purposes. The Author and the publisher are in no way liable for any use or misuse of the material.

Luria, Simon

The Panama Papers: The Largest Financial Scandal of Modern Times

—1st ed

ISBN: 978-1532843327

Printed in the United States of America

Cover images : The temptation of money – © curaphotogra

Book Cover Design: Simon Luria

www.simonluria.com

Source Material and Disclaimer

This series on the Panama papers will constantly be updated with new information.

Please note: All individuals and corporations present in the Panama Papers are innocent until proven guilty. Their existence on the documents does not imply criminality.

Source material and supplemental information is derived from the resources below. I will provide additional sources at the end of the book.

The International Consortium of Investigative Journalists who organized the research of said documents comprising the "Panama Papers." This includes Reports from The Guardian, the BBC, Le Monde, SonntagsZeitung, Falter, and La Nación and German public broadcasters NDR and WDR, and Austrian ORF who were involved in the research and the breaking of this story. The first set of documents, were published on April 3, 2016. More releases are forth coming, including the full list of companies involved in this leak, which is to be released in early May 2016.

This information is presented as is. I make no warranty as to the accuracy of the above reporting sources. I will provide all my sources at the end of the book.

Preface

The term politician has many negative connotations. We assume that if a person is a politician that means they are either corrupt or unscrupulous in some way. To be fair, not all are this way, but many are. The problem is, we always suspect that they are, but we rarely find proof of this. Rarer still, is it to find a politician prosecuted for crimes such as fraud, tax evasion or money laundering. When we do, it makes the headlines because it confirms our deepest suspicions.

And now, yet again, our deepest suspicions have been confirmed. New evidence has come to light that a vast conspiracy exists involving top politicians in the world. Many have been implicated in schemes involving the funneling of money through various hidden schemes to avoid detection. Although some may not be illegal, many are suspicious. Just to be clear, we are not talking only about South American despots, African Tyrants, Middle Eastern strong men and Russian Oligarchs, but also some of the most "esteemed" politicians of our age; the ones we thought were beyond financial fraud and conspiracy. This conspiracy is so far reaching that on April 5th 2016, the Prime Minster of Iceland had to resign because he too was implicated in this conspiracy. Not surprisingly, other prominent people have been implicated as well, such as celebrities, government officials and members of the criminal underground, etc.

The conspiracy is now known as the Panama Papers, a result from a leak of over 11.5 million records describing the alleged fraud of Politicians, Billionaires, Drug smugglers, sports stars and other prominent people in society. It is by far the largest document leak in modern history, outpacing the WikiLeaks and Edward Snowden leaks several times over.

In this book, we will discuss this wide-ranging scandal. There is no doubt at all, this will be the largest financial cover-up ever to emerge in modern times, and we all have a front-row seat to this. Several politicians and prominent people will fall of that we can be certain.

Introduction

Over the past few years, the United States Government has been cracking down on individuals and corporations that shelter money offshore. Banks such as UBS have been fined enormous sums for their role in helping United States citizen's shelter money. Money sheltering, in general, is a gray business, there are legitimate ways to shelter money but for the most part, the governments of the world frown on this practice with very few exceptions. They frown upon it because the sheltering is more often than not used to avoid taxes and in many cases worse things such as covering up extensive money laundering, terrorist activity and drug smuggling activity. What was found in the Panama papers was astounding and a substantial portion of it was found to be of questionable legality.

Much of the controversy involves the use of Shell companies, of which I will get into in greater depth in a future chapter. Corporate shell companies are quite common; companies use them for both legitimate and nefarious purposes. They are mostly used for tax sheltering and like I mentioned above, for illegal purposes. One panama-based law firm, Mossack Fonseca And Co created thousands upon thousands of these kinds of companies for individuals and corporations alike. These shell corporations would otherwise not be traced if they didn't make one crucial mistake. They created over a 1000 of these companies in Nevada. It was this crucial error that ended up uncovering a huge international scandal. It began when prosecutors in Argentina claimed that at least 123 of these companies in Nevada were shell companies used by the former president of Argentina and his associates to rob the Argentinian government of $65 million dollars; not outright mind you, but via government contracts. As a result of the Argentinian Prosecutors investigation, a lawsuit was filed with the U.S. District court of Nevada to undo some of these massive transfers. The courts asked Mossack Fonseca And Co to turn over information regarding these transfers. Generally speaking, it is difficult for the U.S. courts to do this to a foreign entity but this law firm had a Nevada based subsidiary, M.F Corporate Services Limited, this made it easier for the courts to follow through with the lawsuit. However, the co-founder of Mossack Fonseca, Jurgen Mossack, while under oath, denied that M.F, Corporate Services Limited was part of the Mossack Fonseca And Co family of companies. Many found Jurgen's testimony to be shaky at best. Without evidence, not much could be done against Mossack Fonseca And Co and so the lawsuit stalled...That is, until a huge data breach of 11.5 million documents spanning from 1977 to 2015, belonging to Mossack Fonseca And Co was released. They are now referred to as "The Panama Papers."

These documents were analyzed by the International Consortium of Investigative Journalists; this includes close to 400 journalists in 77 countries and was eventually made public by the German news outlet, Suddeutsche Zeitung. What they found was staggering. They were able to find the smoking gun that proved Jurgen Mossack lied under oath, and that they did indeed own a subsidiary in Nevada that helped launder money from Argentina; the rest of the findings started to snowball after that.

Background:

This leak is not only damaging for Mossack Fonseca, but for thousands of individual and corporations who use offshore corporate services. The documents contain over 214,000 names of off shore companies that Mossack Fonseca incorporated in various tax havens around the world, these files include personal information on the beneficiaries of such offshore entities. The release of these documents has caused an uproar throughout the globe. The current global ethos is that of suspicion of the rich and the powerful. These documents showed just how far political types and wealthy individuals will go to hide their wealth and business transactions.

As of the time of this writing, 140 politicians and public servants, including 12 former and current heads of state of Argentina, Iceland, Saudi Arabia, The Ukraine and the United Arab Emirates have been exposed in the Panama Paper leak. Their friends, relatives and close associates have also been exposed. In addition, thousands of other people have been exposed from over 40 countries. Most of the accounts that belong to individuals were housed in the British Virgin Island. Most of the businesses, however, were found to be formed in Hong Kong. More is surely to come, for at the time of this writing, only 150 of the 11.5 million documents have been shared; more is expected in May. These documents include banking records, client records, emails, copies of passports and other personal documents.

The Panama Papers would not have come to light if it was not for an anonymous source known as "John Doe." John Doe released the information in stages to the German News Paper Suddeutsche Zeitung in the beginning of 2015. The total file size was over 2.6 Terabytes of data. To put that into perspective, at current Internet speeds, it would take over 24 hours to download. This leak was too large for Suddeutsche Zeitung to handle on their own, so they called upon the International Consortium of Investigative Journalists for help. They sent pieces of the data to about 400 journalists spanning 77 countries. This includes journalists from The BBC, The Guardian, Le Monde, Falter and many others.

John Doe made it clear that any, and all communications would be using Encrypted Chat since he believed that his life was in danger. It is hard to know his exact motives, but he insisted that he was doing this because he was tired of seeing Mossack Fonseca help known criminals and "doing harm to the world."

Aside from finding and implicating thousands of people and corporations in money sheltering, it also revealed a culture of corruption and subterfuge at Mossack Fonseca itself. It was discovered that they made an organized and concerted effort to destroy as many records as possible that would link them or their clients to anything even remotely questionable; all with the intention of shielding themselves from the long arm of the United States Department of Justice. Such incrementing quotes such as "to be obscure to the investigators." And "tried to clean the logs of the PC's in the Nevada office" were noted.

Mossack's client list was deep and expansive and spanned over 220 countries. Some of these clients were known members of various crime families, drug lords, tax cheats, known terrorists, politically corrupt individuals and black listed companies. What made this so damning for Mossack was that they KNEW that some of these people were criminals and were glad to continue to service those accounts.

In the following chapters, we will discuss in a bit more in depth the history of Mossack Fonseca And Co and about the business of shell companies in general.

The Shell Game

Most countries have regulations in place to control their respective private sectors. These regulations are in place, not only to ensure that the business landscape is not heavily screwed in favor of one group, but also to protect the general economy from the dangerous effects of unmitigated risk. Another major reason is to ensure that the government can collect tax revenue. In many ways, this is the strictest of these regulations since tax evasion will often come with severe penalties that sometimes outweigh the punishment for more serious crimes. In short, you do not want to mess with the government's money; and for a good reason. Tax receipts are used to maintain infrastructure, military spending and other functions that are required to maintain a nation. Ideally, that is where the money is going, often we see that governments are not wise with this money and that causes a ripple effect in the economy at large. Often the mismanagement of this revenue creates obligations that the government is hard-pressed to repay. The money needs to come from somewhere and in most cases of highly leveraged nations, they raise taxes on the citizenry which includes business as well.

For the average person, these tax increases are burdensome and are often unavoidable. When you make just enough to get by, there is no way to shelter money from the taxing authorities.

Individuals making a bit more can shelter some of this tax burden or at least defer it via various legitimate investments; be it retirement funds, varied debt obligations and the like. Then we have another class of an earner whose income and assets are far above the rest of the population, the 1 % as it were (This includes corporate citizens). Unless they are very strategic with the allocation of their respective assets, the tax burden can be substantial. While most very wealthy individuals and corporations mitigate tax burdens legitimately, some do not. There are many ways in which one can avoid taxes, but the one most pertinent to this book is the use of Shell Corporations.

Shell companies can be a rather complex topic. However, for the sake of brevity, we will discuss the two major types here.

Shell Corporations: This form of corporation is one that exists for a very specific purpose. It exists nominally on paper but does not have any employees, assets and does not generate any direct economic output. (Shell companies can also be defunct companies that have maintained their corporate identities). Although they are "shells," the creation of such companies is not illegal. Often they are used to buy certain assets such as other companies, real estate or other assets. It is essentially a vehicle to facilitate business transactions. This corporate shell is ideal in many ways because it is often able to anonymize the true owners. This facet allows for individuals and other corporations to avoid taxes, transfer assets at favorable prices between different corporations abroad. This facet is also quite attractive to those conducting illicit businesses; these unscrupulous operators can hide their identities as they shuttle illegally obtained money throughout the financial system without raising any red flags.

Like all corporations, there is paperwork and various other formalities that need to take place before the corporation can be formed. Often, this formality can be a nuisance to those who are in a rush to hide their financial misdeeds. There is, however, a solution to this and that is buying an existing company to bypass the formalities. That takes us to our next Shell company type.

Shelf Corporations: Shelf companies are the most popular kind of corporation for those who want to facilitate their respective transactions as quickly and as quietly as possible. This form of Shell Company is one that is already created and is simply "shelved" until it is purchased. Often these companies are left on the shelf for a specific period of time, so they can "age." This aging creates the illusion that the company has been established for a long time despite having no economic activity. The beauty of this kind of corporation is that the registration and the formalities are already completed, and thus it is a kind of plug and play company that can be used right away. This is very attractive not only to those who use them legitimately, but to those who need to cover their tracks. This secrecy is further compounded if the corporation was formed offshore in locations with very strict confidentially laws. Couple Shell corporations with these kinds of laws and you have the perfect instrument for deception and anonymity.

Forming a Shell Company for Anonymity:

Individuals or corporations can have shell companies created quite easily. However, in order to take advantage of anonymity, the shell corporation needs to be created in a location that has strict banking secrecy laws and low transaction fees. There are quite a few locations where you can find banking secrecy laws such as the Cayman Islands, Switzerland, Belize, Turks and Caicos and quite a few more. The United States too, has Tax Havens, mainly the states of Nevada and Delaware.

To form a shell company in the Cayman Islands, for example, an intermediary such an individual, bank or company would arrange for the registered agent to create and handle the logistics of the Shell Company for an agreed-upon fee. The registered agent will have people "assigned" to the corporation. These people are, in fact, front people or as the industry calls it "Nominees." These individuals can act as beneficial owners, directors and shareholders of record; this is just a front. These nominees add an extra layer of anonymity so when a transaction is passing through the shell company, the true owner is not revealed. Oddly enough, this practice is not illegal, in and of itself, and that is why it is so problematic.

The reason it is so problematic is because there are legitimate uses for corporations that are based offshore.

A few are:

Investing and holding Property offshore:

There are investment opportunities the world over, including offshore. However, some offshore investment houses and real estate companies may not allow clients from the U.S. to invest with them. There are myriad reasons for this but mostly the concern is they do not want to get tangled up with financial regulators in the states. So to avoid this, a US citizen can form an offshore company and through it, investing offshore is made possible.

Asset Protection:

A U.S. company can protect some of its assets by having them held in an offshore company. Since these offshore havens are not subject to certain lawsuits, the assets will remain protected. This does not exempt the company from paying taxes on those assets, but it does protect them from litigation.

Avoidance of Probate:

In certain cases, an offshore entity can be used to avoid probate. If the offshore corporation is offshore from where the property is located, depending upon the jurisdiction, the direct inheritance of the offshore entity to the beneficiaries may be able to bypass probate.

There are other legitimate reasons to have an offshore entity, but that is a topic for another discussion and beyond the scope of this book.

Regardless of the kind of Shell Corporation one would need, there needs to be a registered agent who files the necessary paperwork to create the corporation. One company was all too eager to be the registered agent of record for the most notorious people and companies on the planet, and it was their records that are now the focus of the entire world. These records are now infamously known as… The Panama Papers.

Mossack Fonseca: The Registered Agent of Record

Those who wish to form or purchase a shell corporation offshore and retain anonymity while doing so has many options to choose from. However, there are five giants in the industry who are most experienced in this line of business; One of them being, Mossack Fonseca.

Ramon Fonseca one of the co-founders of Mossack Fonseca founded his small law firm in 1977. In 1986, he joined forces with a German based Panamanian lawyer Jurgen Mossack. Together they form the now-infamous Mossack Fonseca. From its humble beginning, it is quite astounding that now it boasts over 500 employees and has offices spanning the globe; 40 in total, in which nearly a quarter are based in China. Records dating back to 2013 show $42 million dollars in revenue with at least $ 2 trillion dollars passing through their various companies.

Despite the humble origins of both firms, Jurgen and Ramon were not new to the world of money and power and knew how to leverage their expertise.

Jurgen Mossack was born in Germany in 1948. He received his bachelor's degree in law in 1973 from the Universidad Catolica Santa Maria La Antigua. His father Erhard, was a member of the Waffen-SS, the much rivaled military wing of the Nazi Party during World War II. According to U.S. Intelligence, he offered to be a spy for the United States. In the 1960s, he moved to Panama where he offered to spy on communist activity in nearby Cuba for the CIA. It was confirmed that he did work for the C.I.A, but that is all we know; no other information has been disclosed.

Ramon Fonseca was born in 1952 in Panama and studied political science and law at the London School of Economics and the University of Panama. He was an idealistic young man at the time and hoped to one day "save the world." He even considered the priesthood as a viable life choice. This all changed as he matured, he not only became a successful lawyer and novelist, he also stopped wanting to change the world and in his own words "… As one gets older, you turn more materialistic"… The days of altruistic ideology were gone.

The success of Mossack Fonseca is a reflection of the unbridled ambition of its founders. Since it's inception the firm has managed and created well over 300,000 companies. Several companies on their client list were found to do business with actively sanctioned nations, individuals, despotic dictators and arms dealers.

Key Events That Shaped Mossack Fonseca's Business:

The British Virgin Islands:

The Panama of 1986, in which Mossack Fonseca found themselves in was under the control of the infamous military dictator, Manuel Noriega, who reigned with terror from 1983 to 1989. It was during this time; Mossack Fonseca established its first office outside of Panama; in 1987, they opened an office in the British

Virgin Islands. They did this not to escape Noriega but to exploit the new laws that made it very easy for individuals and Corporations to form offshore entities without revealing who owned them. This law is still very much in place. The British Virgin Islands now holds over 40% of the offshore company market. It is a large portion of Mossack Fonseca's business as well, with over 50% of the companies they created housed there. The number of firms and entities they incorporated there runs between a staggering 100,000 to 113,000; this number represents about half of their total business. Although this seems like a large number, you must keep in mind that, in this industry, Mossack Fonseca is the 5th largest in the world, others have incorporated many times what Mossack Fonseca has and still do.

It was not always smooth sailing in the British Virgin Islands though, in 2012-2013 the island's regulators got wind that Mossack Fonseca was helping people launder money through its banks; one of these individuals was Alaa Mubarak, the son of the former strong man of Egypt, Hosni Mubarak. Mossack Fonseca was fined $37,500 for their involvement.

The Nation of Niue:

In 1994, Mossack Fonseca was going strong and were slowly making a name for themselves. In a significant boost to their business, they became the law office of choice to advise the small nation of Niue in its pursuit to become an offshore financial center. Niue is a small island country in the South Pacific Ocean with population of just over 1100.

Mossack Fonseca was the only law firm advising Niue and ran its offshore business almost exclusively from its Panama offices. Business was so good that Mossack Fonseca was paying $1.6 million of the nation's $2 million annual budget. It's hard to believe that one company could carry the entire Island, but that is exactly what was happening and there was no end in sight. Business continued to grow into the late 90s. However, the gravy train would not last, and things came to screeching halt. American Banks discovered that Niue was starting to become a conduit of criminal activity. In 2001, the banks imposed an embargo on money transfers to Niue, a death blow to its economy. As a result, Mossack Fonseca's business began to dry up, and they were forced to close down their business there in 2005. Accounts that were housed in Niue were eventually transferred to American Samoa, which is also a robust tax haven. The transfer of accounts was seamless and swift.

In the following years, Mossack Fonseca branched out into other lines of business such as investment management. This service was conducted under its corporate name Mossfon Asset Management S.A. Mossack Fonseca yet again displayed their Midas touch and quickly gained success in this arena; processing thousands of transactions and moving well over $1 billion dollars in client funds. Since these operations are all offshore, it was only a matter of time before it would get entangled with financial organizations that conducted shady business such as Banca Privada d'Andorra, and Deutsche Bank Switzerland.

In 2015, The U.S. treasury accused Banca Privada d'Andorra of money laundering for drug lords. Eventually, In 2016, the treasury dropped the charges against Banca. Deutsche Bank Switzerland is not as lucky and is still being investigated in the U.K. and U.S. for helping launder money for Russian Oligarchs.

Mossack Fonseca saw that these high-profile clients needed even more products and services in order to allow them to stay in the shadows. Mossack Fonseca offered other services such as the backdating of important documents. One of the most damning is the creation of fake charities. This helped clients move their money around in the guise of "charity." These services were very attractive to those who had something to hide.

The International Consortium of Investigative Journalists, the organization that analyzed the leaked documents discovered that these services were in high demand by individuals and corporations that were blacklisted by the U.S. department of Justice and the Treasury. Many were blacklisted for their involvement in the drug trade, arms dealings with Iran and other activities the U.S. authorities found to be counter to U.S. interests.

Commerz Bank Scandal:

In 2015, the German government raided Commerzbank for information regarding suspected tax evasion and money laundering. Mossack Fonseca are being investigated for their possible involvement in these schemes.

Petrobras Scandal:

In early 2016, employees of Mossack Fonseca's Brazilian office were charged with their involvement in the never-ending money-laundering Petrobras scandal which entailed artificially inflating fuel prices and using the ill-gotten gains from this activity to enrich themselves, bribe powerful Politicians and Energy Company officials for favorable contracts and rulings. The Mossack Fonseca headquarters stated it had no direct control over its Brazilian offices since it was considered a "franchise" and did not have a say in its activities, which seems unlikely. According to Ramon Fonseca, the firm has since been cleared of these allegations.

Hidden In the Shadows

The fallout from the Panama Papers leak is so expansive it may take another few years before the scope is truly grasped. Mossack Fonseca created Shell companies at such a breakneck pace that it would be impossible, even for the 400 journalists to parse through it all in a short period of time. It took a year just to get to this point and it is simply the tip of the iceberg. As I write this, more and more is being revealed. It is for this reason I am writing this as a series since there is no way to account for every single piece of breaking news as it happens. In this chapter, we will discuss the revelations that have come to light thus far. The information that follows is not complete, more names are being added every day. In future volumes of 'The Panama Papers' series, we will publish the entire list when it is made available. Please note that the individuals and corporations that are mentioned in the Panama Papers and in this book, are not necessarily guilty of a crime. As I stated earlier, there are legitimate uses for offshore accounts.

Please note, this chapter is tightly pack so please bear with me you may also skip this chapter and come back to it later.

Key Highlights:

I will first discuss some of the more important findings before I go through the list of known beneficiaries mentioned in the Panama Papers.

As I stated in the introduction, several heads of state, their families and associates have been exposed in the Panama Papers. Here are the facts as we know them.

The Panama Papers identified at least 60 associates and family members of Kings, Presidents and Prime Ministers, including David Cameron's father, Ian Cameron. I will discuss his case a bit later in the chapter.

Other leaders include: Petro Poroshenko of the Ukraine, King Salman of Saudi Arabia, Prime Minister of Iceland Sigmundur Davíd Gunnlaugsson, who eventually stepped down. (I will discuss him a bit later as well). Azerbaijani President Ilham Aliyev.

Former heads of state include: former Ukrainian prime minister Pavlo Lazarenko, Sudanese President Ahmed al-Mirghani, prime minister of Georgia Bidzina Ivanishvili, Emir of Qatar Hamad bin Khalifa Al Thani, former prime minister of Qatar Hamad bin Jassim bin Jaber Al Thani, and Ion Sturza of Moldova.

Family and associates of the following leaders: the children of Pakistani Prime Minister Nawaz Sharif, the brother-in-law of China's leader Xi Jinping, the son of Malaysian Prime Minister Najib Razak, the nephew of South African President Jacob Zuma, the secretary of Moroccan King Mohammed VI, the grandson of Kazakh President Nursultan Nazarbayev, a contractor of Mexican President Enrique Peña Nieto.

It was also discovered that Rami Makhlouf, cousin of Syrian President Bashar al-Assad, had six offshore corporations created by Mossack Fonseca despite US sanctions indicating it was forbidden to do so since he was on the sanctions list. Other deals that defied US sanctions include: A Virgin-Islands based company called DCB Finance, which was founded by Kim Chol (North Korea) and Nigel Cowie (U.K). The bank was formed to circumvent sanctions against North Korea by allowing Korea Mining And Development Trade Corp to transact illegal arms deals.

The news has reported that no Americans were found in the Panama Papers. This is incorrect, at least 200 passports of Americans were found, and it was revealed that at least 400 clients were Americans; none were of Politicians and was therefore, of no interest to the media. It is telling that American Media has not taken the Panama Papers seriously.

The Panama Papers discovered many other individuals outside the realm of politics that may have conducted shady deals. They include several individuals who were or are still connected to the world governing body that oversees football/Soccer...FIFA. This includes Former President of UEFA, Michel Platini, Former president of CONMEBOL, Eugenio Figueredo, former Secretary-General of FIFA Jerome Valcke as well as Lionel Messi a soccer player from Argentina. The leaks did not only expose these individuals as having offshore accounts, but also revealed blatant conflicts of interest. This prompted a raid on the UEFA offices in Switzerland.

No industry was left untouched in the Panama Papers. Several entertainers from around the world were exposed as well. Such as

Actor Jackie Chan who was shown to have six offshore companies. Several Indian and Latin American entertainers were exposed as well. As you can see, this exposure was far reaching.

Now I would like to list each country that was impacted by the Panama Papers in alphabetical order. I will also provide additional commentary as needed. Please keep in mind that this list is not complete, more information is forth coming on the individuals and corporations on this list.

Algeria:

Two prominent individuals were named in the Panama leaks. Notably, President Abdelaziz Bouteflika and Minister of Industry and Mines Abdesselam Bouchouareb. Le Monde, the French Newspaper exposed the two prominent Algerians in what Algeria called a "Malicious Campaign." A journalist for Le Monde was denied a visa to travel to Algeria to investigate the matter further. Algeria and France already have a strained relationship due to years of French rule. Algeria fought for its independence from 1954 to 1962. This will only heighten the mistrust that already exists between the two nations.

Andorra:

Andorra, considered a tax haven in its own right was implicated as well. Jordi Cinca, Minstar of Finance was exposed as having offshore interests. This revelation may not have serious consequences for Jordi. It will have consequences for Andorra as a whole. With nations moving to blacklist Tax Havens, Andorra is most certainly going to be added to that list.

Angola:

Angola is an oil-rich country that channels much of its profits through Angola's Sovereign wealth fund. However, it has been revealed through the Panama Papers that the fund is not completely transparent as to where the money is going. Some have suggested the $ 5 billion dollars of revenue is being laundered out of the country. This comes as no surprise considering the fund has been haunted by "irregularities" as it were. The Panama Papers revealed a very complex structure of Shell Companies that manage the Angolan funds. We do not have all the information, but it is becoming apparent that illegal activity is occurring within the Angolan Sovereign Wealth Fund. One name that came to light was José Maria Botelho de Vasconcelos, who is the Minister of Petroleum. It will be interesting to see how this unfolds. I suspect money laundering is occurring…Time will tell.

Argentina:

As I stated in the introduction, one of the hardest hit in the Panama Files is Argentina. The Argentine President Mauricio Macri is listed as an owner of a Bahama-based trading company, and it is rumored of one other corporation as well. It is not illegal for him to have such a company. However, it is required for him to disclose this which he failed to do so when he was Mayor of Buenos Aires. On April 7th, the Argentine federal prosecutor opened an official investigation against Mauricio.

Another prominent individual who was exposed was football/Soccer great Lionel Messi. It is said that he formed offshore companies to evade taxes. Lionel and the Messi family are fighting these charges.

Others implicate from Argentina are:

Mayor of Lanus, Nestor Gringetti.

Alessandra Minnicelli, wife of Member of the Chamber of Deputies and former Minister of Planning and Public Investment Julio de Vido.

Daniel Muñoz, assistant to former presidents Cristina Fernández de Kirchner and Néstor Kirchner

Gabriel Schürrer, Argentinian retired defender (Soccer).

Leonardo Ulloa, Argentinian footballer/soccer player.

Argentines Gabriel Heinze, a former footballer/soccer player, who co-owns an account with his mother.

Armenia:

It was reported on April 4th in HETQ Online that the Major General of justice, Mihran Poghosyan has ties to at least three offshore companies. On April 8th, Armenian Transparency International Anti-Corruption Center requested that a formal investigation be opened on the matter.

Australia:

The Panama Papers exposed over 800 Australians who were on Mossack Fonseca's Client list. As a result, the Australian Taxation office has opened a formal investigation into these individuals.

Austria:

Reuters reports that the Panama Papers revealed that one of Austria's top banks and lenders, Hypo Landesbank Vorarlberg was connected to offshores via Liechtenstein. This prompted the CEO of the bank, Michael Grahammer to step down. The bank was under pressure recently as other leaks emerged that it had a connection to Offshores that may have circumvented international sanctions. The Panama Papers were simply the straw that broke the camel's back. Michael Grahammer in a statement stated, "I remain 100 percent convinced that the bank at no point violated laws or sanctions." This story will continue to evolve.

Azerbaijan:

It was revealed in the Panama Papers that the president of Azerbaijan Ilham Aliyev and his family live lavish lifestyles due to their interests in almost every sector of the Azerbaijani economy. From Airlines, food services, Gold mines, mobile phone businesses as well as real estate in Dubai worth an estimated $75 million dollars. This number is a conservative estimate.

Bangladesh:

On April 7, 2016, The Anti-Corruption Commission Bangladesh launched a formal investigation into the individuals and businesses in the Panama Papers for possible tax evasion. This includes four prominent business people: Awami League member Kazi Zafarulla and his wife Nilufar as well as Muhammad Aziz Kahn, Samson Chowdhury and Mohiuddin Monem.

Botswana:

It was revealed that the President of the Botswana Court of Appeal and former Attorney General Ian Kirby had invested in at least seven offshore companies based in the British Virgin Islands. The alleged investments spanned from 2005 to 2009. When asked, Kirby indicated that the companies were not conduits of illegal activities but were simply used to buy, develop and sell Real Estate in the United Kingdom.

Brazil:

Brazil has been in the news as of late and is not stranger to conspiracy. Seven national parties were exposed as having members who own or are beneficiaries of offshore companies registered by Mossack Fonseca. Interestingly enough, the scandal ridden Dilam Rousseff, and her associates were not mentioned in the papers. It was also revealed that the former Supreme Court Judge Barbosa and at least 57 other people also conducted offshore transactions that were not disclosed.

Other people of prominence that were implicated are:

João Lyra, Member of the Chamber of Deputies.

Newton Cardoso Jr, Member of the Chamber of Deputies

Eduardo Cunha, President of the Chamber of Deputies

Joaquim Barbosa, former President of the Supreme Federal Court

Edison Lobão, Member of the Senate and former Minister of Mines and Energy

Willian Borges da Silva, Brazilian footballer for Chelsea.

Cambodia:

Ang Vong Vathana, Minister of Justice was exposed in the Panama papers and is now under investigation by the Cambodian Government as to why his name appears in the Papers. He is the sole Government official mention in the leaks, and special attention is being paid to his dealings. Ang Vong Vathana denies that he has any involvement in offshore companies. The truth will come out sooner rather than later, of that I am certain.

Canada:

The Canada Revenue Agency was ordered by the Canadian government to scour the Panama Papers to see if they can discover any Canadians that may be involved in Tax evasion.

The Royal Bank of Canada and the Bank of Montreal both vowed to investigate the Panama Papers closely to make sure they or their clients have not been implicated. It is unlikely many will be found since Canada has very strict laws regarding offshore transactions. However, it was discovered that at least 378 shell companies were associated with RBC and its affiliates. It will be interesting to see how that evolves.

Canadian Prime Minister Trudeau has denied any involvement and made clear. he has been transparent about his and his family's financial assets.

Others implicated from Canada:

Husband of Senator Pana Merchant, Anthony Merchant.

Chile:

Gonzalo Delaveau, the president of the Chilean Brach of Transparency International was exposed in the Panama Papers and has since resigned his post in shame. Although no proof of illegal activity is present, the fact he was head of the very organization fighting offshore havens is rather ironic.

Other Notable Chileans exposed in the leaks:

Intelligence agency associate, Alfredo Ovalle Rodríguez.

Iván Zamorano, Chilean retired footballer/Soccer player.

China:

China, not surprisingly features quite prominently in the Panama Papers. It was revealed that seven leaders of the Politburo of the Communist Part of China as well as other prominent officials, including Li Xiaolin, daughter of the former premier Li Peng had shell companies in the British Virgin Islands.

It was also discovered that former Communist Party General Secretary Hu Yaobang's son Hu Dehua and Deng Jiagui, the brother-in-law of current General Secretary Xi Jinping also has companies in the British Virgin islands. Other prominent individuals have been implicated as well. The Chinese government as it is want to do when bad news comes out, is actively suppressing any mention of the Panama Papers. Social media and search engine results no longer show any reference to the Panama Papers. Media outlets have been ordered to delete all references to the Panama Papers as well. To save face, China has officially condemned and dismissed the Panama Papers as being part of a smear campaign spearheaded by the west against China.

Others implicated in China:

Zeng Qinghuai, brother of former Vice President Zeng Qinghong

Li Jasmine, granddaughter of former Politburo member Jia Qinglin

Chen Dongsheng, grandson-in-law of former Chairman Mao Zedong

Deng Jiagui, brother-in-law of General Secretary Xi Jinping

Hu Dehua, son of former General Secretary Hu Yaobang

Li Xiaolin, daughter of former Premier Li Peng

Patrick Henri Devillers, French business associate of Gu Kailai, a convicted murderer and wife of the former Minister of Commerce and Member of the Politburo Bo Xilai (No Surprise there)

Lee Shing Put, son-in-law of Politburo member Zhang Gaoli

Jia Liqing, daughter of former Procurator General of the Supreme People's Procuratorate Jia Chunwang and daughter-in-law of Politburo member Liu Yunshan.

Amusingly, Jackie Chan the Chinese actor was also on the list of those with offshore accounts.

Colombia:

The Panama Papers revealed at 850 Colombian citizens with ties with Mossack Fonseca and offshore companies. In 2014, Colombia placed Panama on a blacklist for being a tax haven. Now with nearly 1000 citizens implicated, the National Directorate of Taxes and customs has opened an official investigation.

Some of the more notable figures that have been implicated are:

FARC Peace negotiators Camilo Gómez Alzate, Humberto de La Calle and Frank Pearl.

Camilo Gómez Alzate a a high-profile lawyer and politician.

He appears in the Panama Papers as a partner of the limited company Mossack Fonseca & Co the Colomobia Branch. In 2014, Gómez ran as vice president alongside conservative Marta Lucía Ramírez.

Other Colombians mentioned are senators Juan Samy Meregh Marun and Alfredo Ramos Maya.

Bogotá Councilman Roberto Hinestrosa Rey.

Former Mayor of Sincelejo Jesús Antonio Paternina.

Miguel Silva Pinzón, telecom entrepreneur.

Former Finance Minister Alberto Carrasquilla.

Former Finance Superintendent Augusto Acosta Torres.

Banking and finance lawyer Andrés Florez Villegas.

Businessmen Carlos Gutiérrez Robayo and Luis Alberto Ríos Velilla.

Jorge Milton Cifuentes-Villa, Colombian drug trafficker, head of the Cifuentes-Villa Drug Trafficking Organization and a partner of the now captured, Chapo Guzmán.

Hollman Carranza, son of Colombian emerald mogul Víctor Carranza.

Republic of the Congo:

Jaynet Désirée Kabila Kyungu, Member of the National Assembly and sister of Congolese President Joseph Kabila, has been implicated in the Panama Papers.

She is linked to an offshore Holding company based in the Pacific island of Niue. She has declined to comment.

Other Congolese citizens implicated in the leaks:

Minister of Scientific Research and Technical Innovation and former Chairman of the SNPC, Bruno Itoua.

Cyprus:

Cyprus itself is a Tax haven and Mossack Fonseca has an office there. At the time of this writing, there have been no Cypriote citizens mention in the papers. However, the Central Bank of Cyprus is launching an internal audit to ensure they were not unwitting participants in any tax evasion schemes.

Ecuador:

Several prominent Ecuadorian citizens have been implicated in the Panama papers. Current Attorney General, Galo Chiriboga. Former Central Bank president and cousin of President Rafael Correa, Pedro Delgado. As well as Rommy Vallejo, former director of Ecuador's intelligence service.

It was revealed that Chiriboga and Delgado invested in real estates via offshore companies registered by Mossack Fonseca. Rommy Vallejo was named as a representative of the Quito office of Mossack Fonseca. All involved have either denied wrongdoing or have no comment.

Others implicated in Ecuador:

The former advisor to Rommy Vallejo, Javier Molina Bonilla.

Egypt:

It was discovered that several London-based properties, owned by offshore holding companies below to Hosni Mubarak's son, Alaa Mubarak. I am sure a formal investigation will be opened concerning that the U.K just enacted laws to increase financial transparency.

France:

According to the French paper Le Monde, France's bad boy banker and former head of the International Monetary Fund, Dominique Strauss-Kahn has unsurprisingly shown up within the Panama Papers as a director of Leyne, Strauss-Kahn and Partners or LSK. LSK helps clients establish Tax haven corporations through a Subsidiary called ASSYA Asset Management Luxembourg. It became a subsidiary of LSK in 2013. Dominique Strauss-Kahn told the paper that he did not have involvement in the company's day to day activities.

Another High profile individual, Marine Le Pen, the leader of the National Front (FN) a right-wing Anti-immigration party was also found to have an offshore account as stated in the Panama Papers. In an article for the Financial Times, The National front quickly distanced themselves and stated on the record that the organization itself did not have any involvement in offshore activity.

The French Bank Societe Generale was also mentioned in the Panama Papers, but they have since denied any involvement in any wrong doing.

That, of course is yet to be verified as the leaks continue to trickle.

President Francois Hollande vowed to bring any or all tax evaders to justice. In addition, France blacklisted Panama as a tax haven.

Other French Citizens Implicated in the Leak Are:

Patrick Balkany, Member of the National Assembly and Mayor of Levallois-Perret and his wife Isabelle.

Jérôme Cahuzac, former Minister of the Budget.

Nicolas Crochet, accounting associate of Marine Le Pen, leader of the National Front.

Frédéric Chatillon, business associate of Marine Le Pen, leader of the National Front.

Arnaud Claude, former law partner of former President Nicolas Sarkozy.

Robert Louis-Dreyfus, a French businessman, and owner of Olympique de Marseille.

Waldemar Kita, a Franco-Polish businessman and president of Football Club de Nantes.

Georgia:

Unsurprisingly, it was discovered that Bidzina Ivanishvili, former Prime Minister of Georgia was on the list of those who operate offshore companies. It was revealed that in 2011, he had a major stake an offshore entity called Lynden Management. He made much of his fortune in Metals and the banking industry. Although he flaunts the fact he is a billionaire, he does quite a bit of philanthropic work as well.

Ghana:

The son of Ghana's former President John Agyekum Kufuor has been implicated in the Panama Papers scandal as having offshore interests. He is said to have had a controlling interest in a bank account in Panama worth upwards of $75,000.

The Panama Papers also revealed that his mother – Theresa Kufuor, was also a beneficiary of said account.

Greece:

Some of the more notable Greek individuals implicated in the Panama Papers are Stavros Papastavrou, former

Greek PM Antonis Samaras' closest associate and ally. It was revealed that. Papastavrou was the member of the Board of three offshore entities.

Other Greek Citizens implicated in the leaks:

Konstantinos Lanaras and Spiros Metaxas, both are associated with two offshore companies along with Mr. Papastavrou.

Mr. Papastavrou denies the claims as would be expected. A formal investigation is yet to be announced.

Greece has been in the spotlight for several years now as it pertains to their financial transparency and fiscal solvency. It would not be a surprise if those with the means to do so, would shelter their finances from the crumbling Greek banking system and from the overall political uncertainty that is shrouding Greece in darkness.

Guatemala:

Guatemala was also hit hard by the Panama Papers with 33 individuals and over 1200 companies.

Univision reported that Mossack Fonseca's Guatemalan clients included a company headed by the infamous drug trafficker Marllory Chacón, who was accused of laundering $4 million of drug money through Panama between 2009 and 2010. U.S. Treasury Department described Marllory Chacón as Guatemala's "most active money launderer".

Guinea:

The widow of Guinea's late President Lansana Conte, Mamadie Toure was implicated in the Panama Papers as having power of attorney over the British Virgin Islands Company; Matinda Partners and Co Ltd. U.S. Authorities claimed that Toure received $5.3 million through the company to help a mining company win a mining concession before her husband died.

Honduras:

The Panama Papers implicated César Rosenthal, a member of the extremely wealthy Rosenthal family. A Family mired in legal troubles. The Papers show that Cesar created an offshore company solely dedicated to purchasing an aircraft. This aircraft was inspected and seized by the Guatemalan government for its connection to a drug-trafficking operation. Other members of the Rosenthal family have been indicted in the United States for money laundering so it is no surprise that Cesar is following in their footsteps. The Rosenthal's are essentially a crime family.

Hungary:

Just about every nation has been implicated in the Panama Papers, Hungary is no exception. It was revealed that from 100 or more Hungarians on the list, two former law makers, one from the ruling Party Fidesz and one from the Opposition socialist party have been implicated. Both sides vehemently deny the accusations. Prime Minister Viktor Orban has announced a formal investigation.

Iceland:

From all of European countries implicated in the Panama papers, Iceland was the only one to have a leader stepdown. (I suspect others will stepdown as well).

Reuters reports that on Wednesday, April 6, 2016 Fisheries Minister Sigurdur Ingi Johannsson was appointed as new Interim Prime Minster, until an early election can be called in the fall. Former PM Sigmundur David Gunnlaugsson stepped down as it was revealed that he had offshore accounts that he, and his wife benefited from. The account held several million dollars of Icelandic Bank Debt. This, in and of itself, was not necessarily illegal. What brought him down was that he did not disclose it as required by Icelandic Law. Iceland is incredibly progressive in terms of its financial regulations. Unlike every other country in the world, it prosecuted and jailed bankers for their participation in the 2008 financial crisis that devastated much of the globe. It was believed that the United States was the one that took most of the fallout from the crisis, perhaps if measured in sheer dollars lost. However, I disagree that the United States took the largest hit; Iceland was hit far worse. It destroyed every aspect of the economy, not one person was spared. Once banks failed, people were storing their money under their mattresses and destroying assets, just so they could collect insurance to pay off debts in incurred by their purchase. Iceland has been truly devastated. It came as no surprise that once the Panama Papers came to light that they could take swift action against all those implicated.

Other prominent Icelandic Citizens Implicated are:

Júlíus Vífill Ingvarsson, Member of the Reykjavík City, who has since resigned.

Bjarni Benediktsson, Minister of Finance.

Ólöf Nordal, Minister of the Interior.

India:

Approximately 500 citizens of India have been exposed in the Panama papers. Prime Minster Narendra Modi called for an official investigation of the matter. A multiagency group, including the Reserve Bank of India, the tax and foreign currency authorities as well, the financial intelligence unit will be conducting the investigation.

Others implicated In India include:

Anurag Kejriwal, former president of the Lok Satta Party Delhi Branch.

Harish Salve, former Solicitor General and son of N. K. P. Salve, veteran Indian National Congress politician.

Anil Vasudev Salgaocar, former Member of the Goa Legislative Assembly.

Rajendra Patil, Business person and son-in-law of Karnataka minister Shamanuru Shivashankarappa.

Jehangir Soli Sorabjee, son of former Attorney General Soli Sorabjee.

Zavaray Poonawalla, brother of billionaire Cyrus S. Poonawalla He also heads the managing committee of Royal Western India Turf Club.

Indian businessman K P Singh.

Iqbal Mirchi, the right-hand man of India's most notorious criminal, Dawood Ibrahim.

Rattan Chadha, Indian-born Dutch businessman, founder of Mexx clothing

Indian actor Amitabh Bachchan.

Aishwarya Rai Bachchan, Indian actress and former Miss World

Chairman & Managing Director of Apollo, Tyres Onkar Kanwar

Abdul Rashid Mir, founder and CEO of Cottage Industries Exposition Limited (CIE) & Tabasum Mir.

Shishir Bajoria, Indian promoter of SK Bajoria Group, which has steel refractory units.

Vinod Adani, Indian businessman, elder brother of Gautam Adani, Adani Group.

Indonesia:

Finance Minister, Bambang P.S. Brodjonegoro was one of the first to respond when the Panama Papers were released. This is understandable since Indonesia has been having difficulty discovering tax evaders. If, in fact, the citizens of Indonesia that are named in the Panama Papers have evaded taxes, Indonesia will work aggressively to collect the back taxes and prosecute the perpetrators.

Iraq:

Ayad Allawi, former Acting Prime Minister of Iraq was implicated in the Panama Papers as owning several luxurious properties in London which he bought through a shell company, I.M.F Holdings Inc. The company has since dissolved.

Ireland:

Aside from a few individuals implicated in Ireland, there are 323 companies that are also implicated.

The individuals implicated are

Frank Flannery: A political consultant and Fine Gael's former Director of Organizations and Strategy. The leaked documents show that in 1996, Flannery secured a loan to create rehab centers. He used a company in the British Virgin Islands and its assets as collateral for the loan.

James Stanley: in 1990s, he was part of an investigation that involved shares in a company called Bula Resources plc, which he was chief executive. The Shares worth over €2 million were transferred to a British Virgin Islands company. According to Stanley, the shares were meant as a payment to a Russian company in exchange for participation in a Siberian oil field.

Dermot Desmond, Irish businessman.

Israel:

Israel was hit particularly hard by the Panama Papers leak. Over 600 companies and well over 800 Israeli citizens are listed in the leaks. Named in the leaks are some of the heavy hitters in Israeli society such as Dov Weissglass, one of the leading attorneys in the country. He held a high position in the Hawkish Ariel Sharon Administration. According to the leak, Dov is the sole owner of one of four offshore companies. The other 3 are co-owned by one Assaf Halkin. Weissglass and his partner Halkin told Israeli News Paper Haaretz that the companies were declared, and the required taxes were paid in Israel.

Jacob Engel an African Mining Magnate. Idan Ofer a member of a very wealthy and prominent Israeli family was also listed on documents in the leak.

Others implicated on the Israeli side:

Several unnamed, Bank Leumi representatives and board members.

Yitzhak Abuhatzeira, son of Rabbi David Abuhatzeira and great-grandson of Baba Sali. I just happened to have met David several years ago in Israel when I was in Beersheba.

Jacob Weinroth, a prominent Israeli attorney, and founder partner of Dr. J. Weinroth & Co. Law Office.

Beny Steinmetz, billionaire Israeli businessman, with an extensive portfolio in diamond-mining, engineering and real estate. He was featured in a scathing German documentary which excused him of brining African officials for rights to a diamond mine.

Teddy Sagi, an Israeli billionaire businessman and founder of Playtech and the majority shareholder of Market Tech Holdings, which owns London's Camden Market.

Lev Avnerovich Leviev, an Israeli businessman and owner of Lexinter International Inc., which holds shares in Vauxhall Securities Inc.

Durgham Maraee an Israeli lawyer and owner/CEO of Wataniya Mobile.

Dan Gertler, and Israeli billionaire businessman and the founder and President of the DGI Group of Companies

On the Palestinian side: Tareq Abbas, a son of Mahmoud Abbas, the president of the Palestinian Authority, was also revealed to more than $1 million in an offshore company associated with the Palestinian Authority.

Others on the Palestinian side:

Khaled Osseili, former Mayor of Hebron

Mohammad Mustafa, former Minister of National Economy.

Mohammed Rashid, former advisor and a financial manager to Yasser Arafat.

Italy:

As of the time of this writing all that is known, is 800 Italians citizen were mentioned in the Panama Papers. On April 6th, 2016 the Procura of Turin to investigate the 800 mentioned in the papers.

Others implicated from Italy are:

Silvio Berlusconi, no surprise there.

Nicola Di Girolamo, a former Member of the Senate.

Santiago Vacca, Italian accountant who was appointed by Silvio Berlusconi and Giovanni Toti as coordinator of Forza Italia.

Giuseppe Donaldo Nicosia, convicted of bribery alongside former Senator Marcello Dell'Utri

Silvio Sacchi, a former judge along with his partner Fabio Fraissinet as well as his accountant Salvatore Bizzarro

Stefano Ottaviani and Roberto Ottaviani, both Italian businessmen. Stefano is the son-in-law of Gianni Letta, former advisor to Silvio Berlusconi.

Jarno Trulli, Italian former Formula 1 driver.

Francesco Ambrosione, Italian entrepreneur.

Marco Angelo Angiolini, Italian property developer.

Michele Anti, Italian financial prosecutor.

Gianluca Apolloni, Italian business consultant.

Ercole Astarita, Italian entrepreneur.

Franco Dragone, Italian-Belgian theatre director, known for his work on Cirque du Soleil.

Adriano Chimento, Italian jeweler.

Barbara d'Urso, Italian television actress and singer.

Carlo Verdone, Italian actor, screenwriter and film director.

Simone Cimino, Italian businessman.

Marco Perelli Cippo, Italian businessman.

Luca Cordero di Montezemolo, Italian businessman and politician.

Domenico De Leo, Italian business consultant.

Antonio Daniele, Italian entrepreneur.

Gabriele Benfenati, Italian ship owner.

Salvatore Bizzarro, Italian business consultant.

Giovanni Fagioli, Italian businessman and ship owner.

Alfio Fazio, Italian entrepreneur.

Carlo Fazio, Italian entrepreneur.

Carlo Focarelli, Italian businessman.

Marco Toseroni, Italian businessman.

Gabriele Volpi, Italian-born Nigerian businessman.

Valentino Garavani, Italian fashion designer and founder of the Valentino SpA brand.

Gian Angelo Perrucci, Italian businessman in the oil industry.

Domenico De Leo, Italian accountant.

Ivory Coast:

Jean-Claude N'Da Ametchi a banking executive from the Ivory Coast has been exposed in the Panama Papers. for allegedly helping to fund the corrupt government of former President Laurent Gbagbo. It was discovered that he had an offshore firm in Monaco.

Jordan:

Former Prime Minister of Jordan, Ali Abu al-Ragheb was exposed in the Panama Papers as having three shell companies in the Seychelles as well as a company in the British Virgin Island. To be fair, he did take on these positions after his stint as Prime Minister so it may have very well been above board.

Kazakhstan:

It was revealed that Nurali Aliyev, grandson of President Nursultan Nazarbayev has several offshore assets, including two companies in the British Virgin Islands. It showed that he also hid considerable assets, including a Yacht among other assets. It's Ironic that Aliyev would have an account offshore since he has spoken publicly that he is very much against offshore entities and how they are used to hide assets.

Kenya:

The most prominent name in the leaks is Kenya's Deputy Chief Justice Kalpana Rawal. It was revealed that she was involved in four offshore companies. Two of which she served as director. This will certainly lead to an investigation, according to the Head Of Law Society of Kenya. Although being a board member of an offshore is not illegal. It is, however, not permitted for acting justices to hold offshore bank accounts. We shall see how the investigation unfolds in time.

Malaysia:

Malaysia was particularly hard hit by the Panama Papers leak. The Papers revealed over 2300 individuals, and corporations have offshore companies and bank accounts. Including the Sultan of Johor and the sons of three prime ministers.

"Some of the most notable names among the individuals and entities are Kamaluddin Abdullah, head of Feldspar Holdings and son of former Prime Minister Abdullah Ahmad Badawi; Mirzan Mahathir, son of Mahathir Mohamad; and Mohamad Nazifuddin Mohamad Najib, son of the current prime minister, Najib Razak. Mahathir's brother-in-law, Mohammed Hashim Mohammed Ali, the onetime head of Malaysia's military.

Sultan Ibrahim Ismail of Johor; Abdul Aziz bin Tawfiq Ayman, husband of Bank Negara Governor Zeti Akhatar Aziz; Muhammad Muhammad Taib, former Rural and Regional Development Minister and UMNO information chief, who since has joined the opposition Parti Keadilan Rakyat; and Lim Kok Thay, the current managing director of Genting Group; Abdul Halim Harun, former chief executive of UMW Holdings, one of Malaysia's biggest conglomerates; Sharifuddin Hizan Zainal Abidin, former Group Managing Director of Felda Holdings Bhd; and Khoo Kay Peng, one of Malaysia's richest tycoons and head of MUI Group."

Source of Malaysian names:

http://www.asiasentinel.com/politics/malaysia-panama-papers/

Malta:

The Panama Papers implicated the Minister for Energy and Water conservation, Konrad Mizzi. It was revealed that he had ties with a shell company that did business with a secretive company in Panama via New Zealand...sounds shady to me.

Others implicated in Malta:

Chief of Staff to Prime Minister Joseph Muscat, Keith Schembri.

Mexico:

Several individuals were exposed including the "favorite contractor" of Mexican President Enrique Pena Nieto. Although it is not a crime to own offshore entities, it is a crime if those holdings are not reported to the government. If any of the individuals on the list opened these accounts for the purpose of tax evasion, they will be subject to fines up to 100% as well as 3-9-year imprisonment. Aristóteles Núñez who heads, Servicio de Administracion Tributaria, the government's tax administration stated that the people implicated in the Panama Papers still have a chance to declare their investments without penalty so long as it is before an official investigation is conducted. Compared to other nations, this is a very lenient approach and one I believe is the right one. It encourages people to come forward without fear. Other nations should follow Mexico's lead in their approach, the only one, so far that seems to be moving in this direction is the Internal Revenue Service of the United States.

Others implicated in Mexico:

Drug trafficker and one of the founders of the Guadalajara Cartel Rafael Caro Quintero.

Moldova:

Ion Sturza, former Prime Minister of Moldova was implicated in the Panama Papers; more information is forthcoming.

Morocco:

It has been discovered that the personal assistant to the King of Morroco, Mounir Majidi has offshore interests in the British Virgin Islands. Majidi is head of Morocco's royal family holding company, which has investments in mining, agricultural and telecom businesses. The lawyer for Majidi said: "The two companies to which you refer were created in strict accordance with laws in place, and their existence is available from public registers."

Richard Attias, Moroccan businessman and husband of Cecilia Attias, ex-wife of former French President Nicolas Sarkozy...

New Zealand:

It is yet to be revealed how many New Zealanders were exposed in the Panama Papers. New Zealand's Inland Revenue Department is looking into obtaining details of any or all New Zealanders, who may have offshore accounts associated with Mossack Fonseca. Please keep in mind that New Zealand is also considered a Tax Haven.

Nigeria:

Several Nigerians have been implicated in the Panama Papers The most prominent are Atiku Abubakar, former Vice President and James Ibori, former governor of the Nigeria's Delta State.

Most troubling is Ibori, who had offshore accounts in Switzerland and elsewhere. He was convicted of a $77 Million-dollar fraud in 2012. The fraud was in connection with his involvement in the oil and Gas industry, which for the continent, is quite robust. Despite his conviction, he managed to flee Nigeria for Dubai but was eventually caught. He is serving a 13 year sentence in the United Kingdom.

North Korea:

Considering the abysmal shape the North Korean economy is in, it is no surprise at least some individuals would consider moving assets offshore.

In a surprise twist, it was revealed that British Banker by the name of Nigel Cowie assisted the Pyongyang regime to circumvent sanctions, but more specifically to help them sell arms and acquire the technology to acquire nuclear weapons through offshore holdings and bank accounts.

He and Kim Chol Sam an official with Daedong Credit Bank created the front company DCB Finance Limited that is headquartered in the British Virgin Islands.

Nigel Cowie claims that DCB Finance Limited was created for legitimate purposes and denies any knowledge that illegal activity was being conducted through it.

I am sure, as the leaks are revealed to the world, we will find that many more individual from North Korea will be implicated.

Norway:

DNB, Norway's largest financial services firm was found to have created at least 30 offshore companies. At least 200 of Mossack Fonseca's clients are Norwegian according to the Panama papers.

Pakistan:

Although the Prime Minister himself, Nawaz Sharif is not mentioned in the Panama Papers; his three children Hassan, Maryam and Hussein are. It was revealed that they own four offshore companies between them. Maryam his daughter was the most vocal against these accusations and took to Twitter saying " I do not own any company/property abroad. My brother has made me a trustee in one of his corporations, which only entitles me to distribute assets to my brother Hussain's family/children if needed. Nothing more than what my brother has already explained. The info provided by leaks does not say any wrongdoing involved. Distortion is willful that a couple of media channels using to settle scores." I am sure much more will be revealed as the leaks continue.

The Panama Papers also mentioned the Late Benazir Bhutto as being an owner of an offshore entity.

Others in Pakistan that were exposed in the Panama Papers:

Malik Mohammad Qayyum, Senior Advocate of the Supreme Court and former Attorney General.

Farrukh Irfan, Judge of the Lahore High Court.

Rehman Malik, former Minister of the Interior and former Director General of the Federal Investigation Agency.

Osman Saifullah, Member of the Senate

Salim Saifullah, Member of the Senate and a Pakistan Muslim League faction leader

Anwar Saifullah, Member of the Senate, and former Minister for Petroleum and Natural Resources and as well as for the Environment and Urban Affairs

Humayun Saifullah former Member of the National Assembly

Brothers Aqueel Hassan and Tanwir Hassan, Pakistani businessmen and owners of the Pakistan branch of Pizza Hut's

Gul Muhammad Tabba, Pakistani businessman and Managing Director of Lucky Textiles

Mahmood Ahmad, Pakistani businessman and CEO of Berger Paints

Bashir Ahmed, Pakistani businessman and chairman of Buxly Paints

Sultan Ali Allana, Pakistani businessman and chairman of Habib Bank Limited

Hussain Dawood, Pakistani businessman, Chairman of Dawood Hercules Corporation Limited, Engro Corporation Limited, Hub Power Company Limited, and The Dawood Foundation.

Gohar Ejaz, Pakistani businessman and financier of Channel 24

Abdul Rashid Soorty, Pakistani businessman and owner of Soorty Enterprise

Azam Sultan, Pakistani businessman and Chairman of ABM Group of Companies

Shahbaz Yasin Malik, Pakistani businessman, managing director of Hilton Pharma, and his family

Sadruddin Hashwani, Pakistani businessman and Chairman of Hashoo Group, and his son Murtaza Hashwani

Mir Khalil-ur-Rahman, Pakistani businessman, founder and editor of the Jang Group of Newspapers

Zulfiqar Lakhani, Pakistani businessman and owner of Lakson Group and Express Media Grou]

Ahmed Ali Riaz, son of Pakistani business magnate Malik Riaz Hussain who founded and owns Bahria Town

Shahid Nazir, Pakistani businessman and CEO of Masood Textile Mills

Zulfiqar Paracha, Pakistani businessman and owner of Universal Corporation (Pvt) Ltd.

Panama:

Panama, the center of this entire scandal is reeling from the Mossack Fonseca leak. Countries around the globe are reclassifying it as a tax haven and business is slowly eroding. The government has been so rattled by this that lawsuits are threatened to all those who tarnish the image of Panama.

Panama's Lawyers Movement harshly condemned the attack on Panama. The president of the movement, made it exceedingly clear that this was an attack on the country's financial system. He states," I invite all organized forces of the country to create a great crusade for the rescue of the country's image…." Clearly Panama is in serious trouble both in its reputation and its economy. It will be interesting to see how this will unfold.

Qatar:

The former Emir of Qatar Hamad Bin Jassim bin Jaber Al Thani was implicated in the Panama Papers, It was revealed that he has an estimated Net worth of over $1.2 Billion dollars and houses it in several shell companies.

Peru:

Several prominent Peruvians have been implicated in the Panama Papers. Including, the former head of Peruvian intelligence, Cesar Almeyda. This is not surprising considering that in 2010, he was being investigated due to allegations that he had several offshore bank accounts. These allegations have apparently been proven true.

Also implicated in the Panama Papers is Peruvian presidential candidate, Keiko Fujimori; whose father, Alberto Fujimori, the former Peruvian president, is in imprisoned for embezzlement and corruption. Many of Peru's prominent presidential candidates in this year's election are named in the Panama Papers which is quite telling. This revelation could cause quite disruption in the electoral process. It is expected that more damning information will be forthcoming.

Another notable figure in the Papers is Mario Vargas Llosa, winner of the Nobel Prize in Literature.

Poland:

From the thousands of people revealed, only three Polish names were mentioned in the Panama Papers.

They Are:

Paweł Piskorski former Mayor of Warsaw: He has claimed that his offshore company, which is registered in Panama was idle and eventually liquidated. It is still not clear why he would form such an entity if he did not consider utilizing it. Despite the company being idle, he stated that he was under no obligation under Polish banking laws to disclose offshore activity. His claims are dubious and should be taken with a grain of salt. He was accused of financial corruption in 2006 so it is not a far reach to suspect his offshore company was somehow involved in this.

Marek Profus: Owner of Profus Management, which sells fuel and military equipment. Profus has stated that he has never carried out illegal activities with the companies located offshore.

Mariusz Walter: Co-owner of the ITI Group, he also states that he never conducted any illegal activities with the offshores he was involved with.

Poland's General Inspector of Financial Information Wiesław Jasinski has since called for a formal investigation into the dealings of the three individuals above.

Rwanda:

The Panama Papers Implicated Brig. Gen. Emmanuel Ndahiro, a close confidant of Rwandan President Paul Kagame, of having ties to the British Virgin Islands Company Debden Investments Limited in September 1998. Hatari Sekoko, a former soldier was listed as the company's owner. The company has been inactive since 2010. I am sure we will learn more about this as the leaks continue to be revealed.

Russia:

It comes as no surprise to me that Russian business men and politicians are on this list. Russian Oligarchs and their associates have a long history of using offshore havens to hide their respective financial dealings, many being unscrupulous and shady.

The strong man of Russia, Vladamir Putin is not mentioned in the list directly, but there is no doubt connections can be made to him. Here are the key findings. Those associated with him Include Boris and Arkady Rotenberg, who are the wealthiest construction magnates in Russia. Other billionaires such as Gennady Timchenko, Alisher Usmanov. These, as well as Putin's press secretary's spouse, family members and other billionaires, oligarchs and Putin's old KGB pals.

The most peculiar name on the list is that of famed Russian cellist, Sergei Roldugin. Sergei, besides being Russia's most famous cellist, he is also the Godfather to Putin's eldest daughter. Suffice it to say, they are very close and some would say Sergie is Putin's closest friend and confidant.

The Panama Papers revealed that Sergie had somehow mysteriously acquired $100 million and a 12% stake in Russia's Largest Media Advertising firm. The BBC described these acquisitions as being "Suspicious deals." When Journalists at Novaya Gazeta asked him about his offshore holdings he stated, "I have to take a look and find out what I can say and what I can't... financial matters are "delicate." That statement seriously undermines his innocence.

Putin himself has denied all rumors of corruption and made it clear that he considered this a smear campaign and an attempt to undermine Russia, spearheaded by the west, especially the C.I.A. His Spokesmen Dmitry Peskov called it "Putinophobia." Suffice it to say, even if it turns out that the conspiracy is true, nothing will be done about it, at least not in Russia.

Others Implicated in Russia:

Valeri Karpin, Russian retired midfielder, current coach of FC Torpedo Armavir.

Dmitry Rybolovlev, Russian businessman, president of AS Monaco.

Saudi Arabia:

The King of Saudi Arabia, King Salman and crown prince Muhammad bin Nayef has been shown to have offshore entities. King Salman was shown to have two companies based in the British Virgin Islands which were used to take out loans of excess of $34 million to purchase property in London.

It is not clear what the crown Prince had offshore entities for. I believe this story will continue to evolve, and many more Saudi names will be revealed.

Senegal:

The Panama Papers has implicated former Senegalese Minister, Mamadou Pouye. Pouye is a childhood friend of the son of former President Abdoulaye Wade, and has held prominent political posts during his father's presidency. Karim Wade, Abdoulaye son and

Pouye were arrested 2013 on corruption charges in which Wade, and his associates were discovered to be illegally amassing assets worth upwards of $240 million. In 2008 Pouye employed Mossack Fonseca to open a bank account in Panama, which transacted close to $35 million in business relating to state business.

South Africa:

Clive Khulubuse Zuma the nephew of South Africa's President Jacob Zuma was exposed in the Panama Papers. Clive is a mining mogul. In 2015, a South African court found Zuma liable in the collapse of a gold mining company that led to over a 5,000 job loss. In the Panama Papers, it was revealed that he had several offshore accounts that are suspected of deals that are considered "questionable."

South Korea:

195 South Koreans have been discovered in the Panama Papers so far with more expected. The most notable of these individuals is Ro Jae-Hun, son of former President Roh Tae-woo. The Papers revealed that Ro Jae-Hun allegedly had three offshore companies with complex structures all based in the British Virgin Island.

Roh has denied any wrongdoing and stated they were created legal for "business and personal reasons." The South Koran government will be launching a formal investigation into the matter.

Spain:

The Spanish minister of industry, energy and tourism, José Manuel Soria was implicated in the Panama Papers as having an interest in two offshore accounts. One in the Bahamas and one in the Tax Haven of Jersey. . He has since resigned. Initially, Soria stated he would not appear before Parliament to discuss this issue, but he eventually had to.

Other Spanish Citizens implicated are:

Demetrio Carceller Coll and his sons. He was the son of Demetrio Carceller Segura, Minister of Industry and Commerce at the start of Francisco Franco's dictatorship.

The Thyssen Family: Borja Thyssen, the son of Baronesa Thyssen, prominent art collectors.

The great grandsons of Spain's dictator Francisco Franco; Francisco and Juan José Franco Suelves.

Micaela Domecq Solís-Beaumont, wife of Miguel Arias Cañete, former Spanish Minister of Agriculture, Food and Environment and current European Commissioner for Climate Action and Energy.

Pilar de Borbón, sister of former King Juan Carlos I.

Oleguer Pujol, son of Jordi Pujol i Soley, former President of Catalonia.

Miguel Blesa, Spanish financial officer, banker and president of the board of Caja Madrid from 1996 to 2009.

The Martinón, Spanish family, owners of the Grupo Martinón, hotel company.

Meliá Hotels International's executive Spanish family, the Escarrer.

Alberto Cortina and his cousin Alberto Alcocer, Spanish businessmen. Are the owner of of Grupo ACS, the largest construction company in the world.

Josep Lluís Nuñez, Spanish businessman.

The Riu, Spanish family, owners of RIU Hotels & Resorts.

Àlex Crivillé, the former Grand Prix motorcycle road racer.

Agustín and Pedro Almodóvar, both Spanish film producers and directors.

Spanish Actor, Imanol Arias.

Marina Ruíz Picasso, granddaughter to Spanish painter, Pablo Picasso.

Singapore:

As of the time of this writing, there have been no Singaporean Citizens exposed in the Panama Leaks. In a joint statement, the Monetary Authority if Singapore and the Ministry of Finance stated, "Singapore takes a serious view on tax evasion and will not tolerate its business and financial centre being used to facilitate tax-related crimes. If there is evidence of wrongdoing by any individual or entity in Singapore, we will not hesitate to take firm action"

Sudan:

The late, Former President of Sudan, Ahmed al-Mirhagni were one of those implicated in the Panama Papers. It was shown that he was the owner of a Shell company based in the British Virgin Island, which had conducted several real estate deals in London. His net worth was estimated to be around $2 million.

Sweden:

On April 4, 2016 the Swedish Financial Supervisory Authority announced that it had initiated an investigation into the financial dealings of Nordea, one of the largest financial firms in the region. Other banks such as Handelsbanken, SEB and Swedbank are also being investigated. However, The Panama Papers showed that Nordea helped to create close to 400 offshore corporations for its high net worth clients and is therefore, the center of the investigation. Nordea is no stranger to these dealings. In 2015, it was fined 5 million euros to settle "Serious Deficiencies" in the way the institution monitored and handled suspected Money-Laundering transactions.

Others implicated from Sweden:

Frank Belfrage, former State Secretary for Foreign Affairs.

Mattias Asper, Swedish retired goalkeeper (Soccer)

Syria:

Syrian politicians and their allies have always been suspected of owning offshore entities. Not only to loot the country, but to conceal its military objectives. It is no surprise that we find Syrians on the Panama Papers list, especially now that the country is in all-out civil war, war and sanction have been enacted.

Some Notables are:

Billionaire brothers Rami and Hafez Makhlouf, who happen to be cousins of Strongman, President Bashar al- Assad. They are incredibly influential and are said to control up to 60 percent of the Syrian economy. They still hold this commanding presence despite being under U.S. sanctions since 2007. They mitigated the bite of the sanctions by forming offshore companies through Mossack Fonseca. It was the ability to avoid the sanctions that have allowed Syria to fund its civil war in which thousands of innocence have been killed.

Thailand:

The Bangkok Post reported that the Anti-Money Laundering Office was seeking information on 21 Thai Nationals as potentially conspiring to evade taxes. This number seems odd since at least 780 individuals, and 50 Thai-based companies have been implicated in the Panama Papers. At least 2 of the companies are considered some of the largest in Thailand, Mainly Phatra Finance and Bangkok Land. It will be interesting to learn why only 21 people are being investigated. I suspect these individuals were on the radar long before the Panama Papers and so the authorities were more than ready to pounce on any evidence against them. We shall see how this evolves.

Tunisia:

The Panama Papers revealed that several Tunisian political figures used Mossack Fonseca to establish offshore entities. The details are still not known. The Tunis Trial Court Prosecutor has opened an official inquiry as did the Tunisian Assemble of the Representatives of the People.

Turkey:

As of the time of this writing, no political figures have been exposed in the Panama Papers. This may change of course. Those who were implicated were all retired Soccer players.

They are: Nihat Kahveci, Tayfun Korkut, and Darko Kovačević.

Ukraine:

For decades, there has always been rumors that the elite of Ukraine have used offshore accounts to shield money. It appears those rumors are true, at least in the case of Ukrainian President Petro Poroshenko. In 2014 while he ran for office, he vowed that he would sell his candy business, Roshen in order to avoid conflict of interest. In was revealed that within a month of that promise, he hired Mossack Fonseca to form an offshore company in the British virgin island which would become the effective owner of Roshen. This move allowed him to evade taxes to the tune of a few million dollars. His actions were in clear violation of Ukrainian law. Not so much for the forming of the company, but for not disclosing it and paying the required taxes. The irony of all this is that his government campaigned very hard against offshore the formation of offshore companies. I am sure we will hear much more about this as the leaks continue to trickle in.

Other implicated in the Ukraine Are:

Former Prime Minister of Ukraine, Pavlo Lazarenko.

United Arab Emirates:

As I stated earlier, it was revealed that UAE president Khalifa bin Zayed Al Nahyan owns real estate in London through a structure of roughly thirty shell companies that Mossack Fonseca had set up for him. By the end of 2015, the shares of those companies were structured as a trust with himself, his wife and children as beneficiaries.

United Kingdom:

Depending on who you ask, one of the biggest bombshells to explode went off in the United Kingdom.

Already embattled David Cameron was fighting even harder for his political life when it was discovered that his father Ian Cameron shielded much of his wealth offshore using Mossack Fonseca's services to evade taxes in the United Kingdom. David Cameron, a staunch supporter of financial transparency initially claimed that he did not benefit directly from these offshore entities. However, that turned out to be untrue. In an abrupt about-face, David Cameron admitted on April 8th 2016 that he made 30 thousand pounds from his father's trust. In addition, The Financial Times revealed that a letter existed from David Cameron to Herman van Rompuy the president of the European Council, requesting that those who benefit from trusts not be named. This was of course was explained away.

I suspect this story is not over. David Cameron has been under so much pressure at home regarding membership in the EU that it is unlikely the press will back down now.

David Cameron was not the only one implicated in the Panama Papers, it was also revealed that six members of the House of Lords have offshore businesses as well AND several of those Lords, and commons were contributors to Cameron's Political Party.

The 4 names released are:

Tony Baldry, former Member of the House of Commons

Michael Mates, former Member of the House of Commons

Michael Ashcroft, retired member of the House of Lords.

Pamela Sharples, Member of the House of Lords

Others Implicated from the U.K.:

Mark Thatcher, son of former Prime Minister Margaret Thatcher.

Sarah Ferguson, former wife of Prince Andrew

David Sharples, son of Baroness Pamela Sharples

Andy Cole, English former footballer (Soccer Player).

Nick Faldo, English professional golfer on the PGA European Tour, now mainly a Golf Analyst.

Simon Cowell, the English reality television judge, business man, philanthropist and media producer.

Stuart Thomson Gulliver, British banking business executive and the current Group Chief Executive of HSBC

Anthony Gumbiner, British businessman, chairman of The Hallman Group

Heather Mills, British environmentalist and entrepreneur.

Soulieman Marouf, British-Syrian businessman.

Gordon Parry, a property dealer who laundered money from the Brinks-MAT robbery through a shell company.

Since this revelation, David Cameron introduced transparency legislation to battle such opaque business dealings. This will only get uglier as time passes.

United States:

From the various journalist groups involved in the analysis, the only United States-based Media group that is involved is the McClatchy Newspapers.

As of the time of this writing, the United States has been relatively unscathed by the Panama Paper leaks. It was discovered that several Americans were implicated, 4 of whom were convicted or accused of financial fraud in the past. As of the time of this writing, no political figures have emerged in the leaks. There are several possible reasons for why Americans do not feature prominently in the Panama Papers; I will discuss those in a separate chapter. We must keep in mind that we are still in the early stages of this leak, and more Americans may be uncovered. The Editor of Suddeutsche Zeitung, the German media outlet that broke the story said, "Just wait for what is coming," implying more Americans might be implicated. Things could get interesting. In response to the Panama Papers, the I.R.S. (Internal Revenue Service) the Taxation arm of the United States Government stated that they would show leniency if Americans come forward now and declare any tax haven assets they may have before they find them in the Panama Papers. A very similar approach to Mexico on this issue.

Other Americans Implicated in the Leak:

Bobby Fischer, the former chess Master.

David Geffen, media business mogul, producer, entertainment executive, philanthropist and co-founder of DreamWorks.

Stanley Kubrick, an American award-winning filmmaker

Igor Olenicoff, an American billionaire.

Marianna Olszewski, American financial author and financial life coach.

Benjamin Wey, a Chinese American financier and president of New York Global Group.

Uruguay:

The Panama Papers have implicated several Prominent Uruguayans.

Notably:

Juan Pedro Damiani, a Uruguayan member of the FIFA Ethics Committee. He has since resigned.

Daniel Fonseca, former footballer/Soccer player. He is now a Sports agent.

Diego Forlán, another Uruguayan soccer player who plays for Peñarol, as well his mother Pilar Corazo and Brother Pablo have all been implicated.

Venezuela:

Venezuela's economy is crashing down due to mismanagement and falling oil revenue. Corruption is also quite prevalent that it is no surprise that several prominent Venezuelans would be involved in offshore transactions.

The Panama Papers implicated the former top military officer Victor Cruz Weffer. Jesús Villanueva, former Director of PDVSA and Adrián José Velásquez Figueroa, former security chief of Miraflores Palace. All of whom worked at the presidential palace during the administration of the late President Hugo Chavez.

President Maduro promised Thursday to investigate any wrongdoing exposed in the Panama Papers.

Zambia:

Zambia's, former Ambassador to the United States, Atan Shansonga was implicated in the Panama Papers as having conducted business in Companies based offshore. Shansonga is no stranger to controversy and allegation.

He was arrested in 2002 in connection to an investigation into the diversion of several million of dollars out of Zambia when the Corrupt President Frederik Chiluba was in office.

In 2004, Shansonga fled Zambia after being accused of receiving "misappropriated monies" and using offshore accounts to launder it.

It is apparent that this scandal travels far and deep into every country on the planet. The above list is by no means complete, in fact, it is only the tip of the iceberg. In future volumes of "The Panama Papers," I will provide updated information as it is released.

Mossack Fonseca - The Response

Since the Panama Papers have been released, Mossack Fonseca has been under increasing amount of pressure and scrutiny. As of the time of this writing, at least three offices of Mossack Fonseca have been raided.

On April 9th, 2016, authorities in El Salvador raided Mossack Fonseca's local office and seized everything they could find. This raid was not initially planned until Mossack Fonseca took their office sign down the day before. This caused the authorities to become suspicious and led the Attorney general Douglas Melendez to order the raid. As is usual fashion, Mossack Fonseca claimed it did nothing wrong, and that it was simply moving offices and therefore, removed the sign. The Salvadorian authorities interviewed employees, removed 20 computers and an unspecified number of documents from the office. No one was arrested.

On April 11th, 2016, At least 20 tax officials working in concert with Peruvian Authorities scoured the local office of Mossack Fonseca, seizing many accounting records of various clients in an investigation into possible tax evasion and fraud.

On April 12th, 2016, local Panamanian authorities in cooperation with organized crime units raided the headquarters of Mossack Fonseca. They removed computers and documents in connection with the leaks.

In the weeks and months ahead we can expect that more offices will be raided, and more information will be revealed. I will follow these developments as they occur in future volumes of "The Panama Papers."

Despite the leaks and the raids, Mossack Fonseca has defended their business. I will provide, in its entirtey, the official response of Mossack Fonseca as released by their Public relations director Carlos Sousa.

"We cannot provide responses to questions that pertain to specific matters, as doing so would be a breach of our policies and legal obligation to maintain client confidentiality. However, we can confirm the parties in many of the circumstances you cite are not and have never been clients of Mossack Fonseca.

We provide company incorporation and related administrative services that are widely available and commonly used worldwide.

It is legal and common for companies to establish commercial entities in different jurisdictions for a variety of legitimate reasons, including conducting cross-border mergers and acquisitions, bankruptcies, estate planning, personal safety, restructuring and pooling of investment capital from different jurisdictions in neutral legal and tax regimes that does not benefit or disadvantage any one investor.

Our services are regulated on multiple levels, often by overlapping agencies, and we have a strong compliance record.

In addition, we have always complied with international protocols ... to assure as is reasonably possible, that the companies we incorporate are not being used for tax evasion, money laundering, terrorist finance or other illicit purposes.

We are responsible members of the global financial and business community.

We conduct thorough due diligence on all new and prospective clients that often exceeds in stringency the existing rules and standards to which we and others are bound.

Many of our clients come through established and reputable law firms and financial institutions across the world, including the major correspondent banks, which are also bound by international "know your client" (KYC) protocols and their own domestic regulations and laws.

Your reporting show that we routinely deny services to individuals who are compromised or who fail to provide information we need in order to comply with our KYC and other obligations.

For 40 years Mossack Fonseca has operated beyond reproach in our home country and in other jurisdictions where we have operations. Our firm has never been accused or charged in connection with criminal wrongdoing.

However, we are legally and practically limited in our ability to regulate the use of companies we incorporate or to which we provide other services.

We are not involved in managing our clients' companies. Excluding the professional fees we earn, we do not take possession or custody of clients' money, or have anything to do with any of the direct financial aspects related to operating their businesses.

All of the jurisdictions where we have operations have made significant strides in their efforts to comply with global protocols to prevent abuse of their financial and corporate systems. This includes preventing money laundering, combatting terrorist financing and preventing tax evasion.

Most of the jurisdictions have formal tax information exchange agreements with several countries that are approved by the Organisation for Economic Cooperation and Development (OECD).

We regret any misuse of our services and actively take steps to prevent it.

We regret any misuse of companies that we incorporate or the services we provide and take steps wherever possible to uncover and stop such use. If we detect suspicious activity or misconduct, we are quick to report it to the authorities. Similarly, when authorities approach us with evidence of possible misconduct, we always cooperate fully with them.

With regards to some of the allegations, we would like to comment as follows:

Tax evasion and avoidance: we strongly disagree with any statement implying that the primary function of the services we provide is to facilitate tax avoidance and/or evasion.

Due diligence on clients: approximately 90% of our clientele is comprised of professional clients, such as international financial institutions as well as prominent law and accounting firms, who act as intermediaries and most of them are regulated in the jurisdiction of their business.

Most of the persons mentioned by you are not our clients nor do they appear in our database as persons related to the companies we formed. Due diligence procedures were carried out in accordance with the laws in place at the time the companies and cases you made reference to were incorporated and in existence.

A significant percentage of our clients are banking institutions, trust companies, lawyers, and accountants who are also obliged to perform due diligence on their clients.

Politically exposed persons (PEPs): we have duly established policies and procedures to identify and handle those cases where individuals either qualify as PEPs or are related to them. As per our risk based approach, PEPs are considered to be high-risk individuals. PEPs do not have to be rejected just for being so; it is just a matter of proper risk analysis and administration.

Sanctions lists and convicted criminals: our company does not foster or promote unlawful acts.

We have our own procedures in place to identify such situations, to the extent it is reasonably possible. Once these types of situations are identified, we routinely discontinue the provision of our services.

The time it takes for us to resign as registered agent from the involved companies varies depending on our internal procedures and the regulations of the respective country or jurisdiction. Sometimes the authorities require the registered agent not to file any resignation in order to prevent obstructing their investigation.

We would like to take this opportunity to clarify that we have never knowingly allowed the use of our companies by individuals having any relationship with North Korea, Zimbabwe, Syria, and other countries mentioned by you that might have been considered as a threat to any other country's national security or that have been listed by a sanctioning body.

If for some reason, unbeknownst to us, some company formed by us ended up in the hands of people having such relations for whatever criminal or unlawful purpose, we strongly condemned that situation and took and will continue taking any measures that are reasonably available to us.

Allegations that we provide shareholders with structures supposedly designed to hide the identity of the real owners are completely unsupported and false.

We will not answer any questions related to private information regarding our company founding partners as we do not see the public interest behind said inquiries. Likewise, we will not make any reference to the statistics and other "factual" information about numbers and amounts since they are far from being accurate. In relation to our asset management company, same does not have the capacity by law to use, move, or dispose of in any way their clients' money.

You may consider this document as our response. However, it should not be considered as a validation of the information contained therein, and especially to the method by which said information was obtained.

It appears that you have had unauthorized access to proprietary documents and information taken from our company and have presented and interpreted them out of context. We trust that you are fully aware that using information/documentation unlawfully obtained is a crime, and we will not hesitate to pursue all available criminal and civil remedies.

Kind regards

Carlos Sousa

Public relations director

Mossack Fonseca & Co. (Panama)

(Letter Obtained from the Guardian Service.)

As would be expected, the company has denied all wrong doing and in some instances, I am sure they were not knowingly involved in any of the schemes which would be considered illegal. I was able to find an internal memo from Jurgen Mossack displaying dismay that a local office did not do its due diligence on a client. This was not an email of complicity but of concern.

https://cryptome.org/pp-mf/cpi/160404-sanctions-02-cpi-16-0403.pdf

It is yet to be revealed if, in fact, Mossack Fonseca has any direct involvement in any crime.

The Oracle of Brooklyn?

If you watch mainstream news, it is apparent that the Panama Papers leaks took most people by surprise. The outpouring of shock and disgust is quiet, well, shocking. It is as if no one ever suspected that these kinds of deals are occurring. The thing is, the proof has been right under everyone's noses, but no one was looking. Could we have avoided this huge mess? Maybe, maybe not, but there was one person who thinks we could have.

In 2008, Senator and presidential hopeful, Bernie Sanders argued against entering a trade agreement with Panama. And again, in 2011, he told the Senate that Panama is "a world leader when it comes to allowing large corporations and wealthy Americans to evade US taxes." His words seem so prescient now. Let us dig deeper into what he exactly said that should have raised red flags.

Bernie Sander, 2011 Speech Transcript:

"Panama's entire annual economic output is only $26.7 billion a year, or about two-tenths of 1 percent of the U.S. economy. No one can legitimately make the claim that approving this free trade agreement will significantly increase American jobs. Then, why would we be considering a stand-alone free trade agreement with Panama, tiny little country?

Well, it turns out that Panama is a world leader when it comes to allowing wealthy Americans and large corporations to evade U.S. taxes by stashing their cash in offshore tax havens. And the Panama free trade agreement will make this bad situation much worse. Each and every year, the wealthiest people in our country and the largest corporations evade about $100 billion in U.S. taxes through abusive and illegal offshore tax havens in Panama and in other countries. So, according to Citizens for Tax Justice—and I quote—"A tax haven ... has one of three characteristics: It has no income tax or a very low-rate income tax; it has bank secrecy laws; and it has a history of non-cooperation with other countries on exchanging information about tax matters. Panama has all three of those. ... They're probably the worst."

Although Senator Sanders could not have anticipated the Mossack Fonseca Leak, he did predict that to allow such a trade deal would make the use of Panama as an offshore tax haven much more attractive. Despite referring specifically to Wealthy Americans and Corporations, his words ring true on a global scale.

The trade deal did pass eventually. It makes you wonder if it passed because those same individuals and corporations that would benefit the most from this deal, lobbied for its approval. I venture to say that the answer is most likely a resounding yes!

Are Rumors Just Unconfirmed Facts?

This book would not be complete without a good dose of conspiracy theory thrown into the mix. It's practically un-American not have at least one or two conspiracy theories for very scandal involving the rich and powerful. The Panama Papers is certainly no exception. Although Conspiracy theories have always been entertained, it was not until the aftermath of 9-11 that they started to gain traction. So many conspiracy theories abounded as to what really happened on 9-11 and whether or not it was an inside job. Universal suspicion of the elite has been in place ever since. With the advent of YouTube and the Internet in general, it is very easy for conspiracies to take hold and disseminate like a fast-moving virus. Do real conspiracies exist? Surely they do; however, not every single event involving the elite is a conspiracy. In this chapter, we will discuss some of the more popular conspiracy theories gaining traction regarding the Panama Papers leak. I will ignore the more outlandish ones such as those that state the government is run by a reptilian alien race and that the Panama Papers are just a distraction for the masses. I can entertain a good conspiracy, but I certainly won't entertain that.

One of the most popular conspiracy theories on the Panama Papers is one perpetrated by many of the same people who believe 9-11 is an inside job.

The Soros Connection:

For some, it has been quite suspicious that the ones implicated in the Panama Papers just happen not to agree with the Polices of the United States. Such as Syrian Strongman Bashar Al-Assad, Russian President Vladimir Putin and Iceland's President Sigmundur David Gunnlaugsson.

Conspiracy theorists the world over despise George Soros, they believe that he, almost singlehandedly is guiding the world into what they call "The New World Order." Not exactly the new world order President Bush Senior referred to in his now famous "1000 points of light" acceptance speech, but a much more ominous one. This is an order ruled by the wealthy elite with the sole purpose of controlling the masses to enrich themselves.

George Soros, the billionaire, Philanthropist, Philosopher and trader is famous for his risky currency trades that can make or break entire nations. He is an unabashed liberal and supports liberal causes around the world through his Open Society Foundations. The outfit that is analyzing and that subsequently helped reveal the Panama Papers is the ICIJ or the The International Consortium of Investigative Journalists. On their about page, they list their various supporters. One of them being Soros's Open Society Foundation. This was enough to cause some to tie Soros directly to the leaks. In fact, they go on to say that he DIRECTLY ordered the leaks to occur. Personally, this is not enough evidence to prove that Soros himself had anything to do with the leaks. Many others also fund the ICIJ, why couldn't it be them? These are questions that the conspiracy theorist cannot answer, just because a high profile individual donates to a cause does not immediately implicate them in a scandal. In the NYC gubernatorial election, I voted for Eliot Spitzer, does that mean I condone prostitution? No, it does not. Support of an organization or individual is not proof of complicity with said individuals or corporations.

They state that Soros's reason to leak these documents is to punish those who are against the polices of the United States; especially Vladimir Putin. Putin has been a throne in the side of the western establishment since he took office but especially since he annexed Crimea in March of 2014. As a result of his actions, he has been sanctioned by the United States and various countries in Europe. This has put a palpable strain on the Russian economic system. Despite the pressure, Putin has remained defiant. His defiance has brought him much scorn from the international community but also much praise from the Russian people. His popularity has only gone up since the annexation. Now that he has been implicated indirectly in the Panama Papers, it has shown a spot light on Putin and his financial dealings. In essence, it is said that the leaks were partially meant to put pressure on Putin and undermine Russia. I suspect this will have very limited impact on Putin or his cronies that are implicated in the leak. It certainly seems like the mainstream Russian Media have largely brushed it off. Unless something incredibly damning is revealed in the leak, Russia and Putin will go about business as usual.

If the leak was meant to target mostly enemies of the United States, why is it that allies such as David Cameron and Sigmundur David Gunnlaugsson are also implicated? This is an inconvenient question for conspiracy theorists. However, an answer is provided.

David Cameron was essentially collateral damage, and his downfall would be an acceptable price to pay if they can take down Putin. These are the conspiracy theorist's words, not my own. Other conspiracy theories suggest something a bit different. David Cameron has questioned the U.K.s membership in the E.U. This has caused quite a bit of unrest domestically as well as throughout the EU. Some have suggested in order to stop David Cameron from pulling out of the EU, it would be best to remove him from office, and a scandal would be the best way to do this.

Some of these conspiracies also state that Sigmundur David Gunnlaugsson was collateral damage as well. However, a much more interesting theory is nested within the larger conspiracy of Soros's involvement. Iceland, under Gunnlaugsson has done something that no other nation has. It jailed the bankers who toppled the Icelandic Economy. No other western nation has taken any direct action against any of the bankers involved in the economic crisis of 2007-2008. The theory goes that his action against the bankers was a hostile act against the banking elites in general, and his implication in the Panama Papers was revenge. This is quite a convoluted theory, but it is out there.

For more information on this conspiracy theory, please visit the links below, they go into great detail:

https://dailymedia.info/john-mcafee-exposes-enormous-panama-papers-hoax/

http://dailycaller.com/2016/04/06/wikileaks-goes-full-kremlin-accuses-us-and-soros-of-funding-putin-panama-papers-leak/

http://www.Infowars.com

Youtube Videos:

https://www.youtube.com/watch?v=qNKAt3DxZXo

https://www.youtube.com/watch?v=_L86THwtNf0

The CIA Connection; Conspiracy # 1:

In the same links above it goes into some detail as to how the C.I.A colluded with Soros into bring the Panama Papers to light. On the ICIJ's about page, it states that the Ford Foundation is also a financial backer. The Ford Foundation, headquartered in New York is a private foundation dedicated to advancing various humanitarian causes. Its link to the C.I.A was started when The foundation's Chairman, John J. McCloy (1958-1965) knowingly employed several C.I.A agents based upon the premise that they were inevitably going to be working with them in some way in the future. The book "The CIA and the Intellectuals" by Jason Epstein discusses this further. In addition, in 1976, A U.S. congressional investigation revealed that about 50% of the 700 grants in the field of internal; activities were funded by the C.I.A via various foundations, the Ford Foundation being one of them. The above is one reason conspiracy theorists contend, that via the Ford Foundation, they pulled off this huge leak. Again, it is only circumstantial and cannot be full confirmed that this was a coordinated effort.

The CIA Connection; Conspiracy # 2:

As I stated earlier in the book, Jurgen Mossacks father, Erhard Mossack was a member of the Waffen-SS during World War 2. According to Us intelligence reports, Erhard offered to Spy for the Americans after the war. Here is a link to one of the now declassified FBI documents referencing Erhard Mossack and his willingness to spy for the U.S.A https://cryptome.org/pp-mf/nyt/Erhard-Mossack-NationalArchives-icij-nyt-16-0406.pdf

In light of this, it seems counter intuitive that this would tie the C.I.A to the Panama Papers since this would mean that Jurgen Mossack, one of the founders of Mossack Fonseca had a hand in it, essentially destroying his own business.

Additional Information can be found at:

http://www.zerohedge.com/news/2016-04-03/mossack-fonseca-nazi-cia-and-nevada-connections-and-why-its-now-rothschilds-turn

The CIA Connection; Conspiracy # 3:

The Conspiracy theorists jumped on the fact that so few prominent Americans were implicated in the Panama Papers. This leads them to believe that since this was an American funded leak, it would not implicate fellow Americans. First of all, this is not true; Americans have been implicated, and as I stated earlier in the book, the ICIJ implied more Americans would be revealed. We must remember only a few hundred documents have been made available. There are 11.49 million documents yet to be released.

There are other potential reasons why Americans may not be on the list. The more likely reason is that the United States itself makes it very easy to form Shell companies, so there would be no need for American Citizens to use these offshore entities. Another plausible reason is that Mossack Fonseca simply didn't do much business with Americans in general. Ramon Fonseca, co-founder of Mossack Fonseca said it himself that the law firm prefers not to have American Clients. Fonseca stated to the Associated Press "My partner is German, and I lived in Europe, and our focus has always been the European and Latin American market... as a policy we prefer not to have American clients."

For background information, please read the article at:

http://www.breitbart.com/national-security/2016/04/08/founder-panama-papers-firm-prefer-not-american-clients/

The Russian Conspiracy:

In an interesting twist and one that runs counter to the prevailing theories is that Russia was behind the Panama Papers, not the C.I.A or Soros. As stated previously, these leaks will not change anything in Russia, and it will certainly not hurt Vladimir Putin, it might only make him stronger.

The Brookings Institute in an April 7th 2016 article posited the idea that perhaps it was Russia behind the leaks. The premise of the article is interesting.

Considering that Putin will not be impacted by the leaks, it is conceivable that Russians released it because it would be far more damaging to the West than it would be for him. If anyone was damaged by this leak, it was the "model" western democracies.

The article states that perhaps ... "The Russians threw out the bait, and the United States gobbled it down. The Panama Paper stories run off Putin like water off a duck's back. But they have a negative impact on Western stability."

The articles went on to say that Russian Intelligence has the exceptional ability to hack into organization rather easily. The hacking of Mossack Fonseca would be an easy thing for them to do. Mossack Fonseca did say that the leak was "not an inside job" and that they were hacked. This is not surprising to me because among the documents that were released, I found a document from an outside auditor stating that Mossack Fonseca failed on all counts as it pertains to customer information security. To view the 2014 audit, please go to:

https://cryptome.org/pp-mf/cpi/160404-sanctions-01-cpi-16-0403.pdf

This audit coincided with the initial release of the leaks as well. Two weeks after this audit, the German press was notified by John Doe that these documents were available. I am not implying the auditor leaked them, what I am saying is that Mossack Fonseca just failed an audit regarding information security just before the leaks, illustrating just how easy it probably was to hack Mossack Fonseca's files.

Although the above audit was not mentioned in the Brookings article, I felt that it tied in nicely with their possible theory as to a Russian-led operation to leak the documents.

Another interesting idea discussed in this article is that it could also be Russia's way of gaining an advantage. As I stated, few American names were revealed, at least not yet. Essentially, Russia might be using the Panama Papers as a blackmailing device. As the article states " I suggest that the purpose of the Panama Papers operation may be this: It is a message directed at the Americans and other Western political leaders who could be mentioned but are not. The message is: "We have information on your financial misdeeds, too. You know we do. We can keep them secret if you work with us." In other words, the individuals mentioned in the documents are not the targets. The ones who are not mentioned are the targets."

I find this possible reason for the leak quite compelling. In the end, the burden of proof is on those making the claim. Until these conspiracy theories are proven true, they will remain just that... Conspiracy Theories.

To read the entire Brookings Institute article, please go to:

http://www.brookings.edu/blogs/order-from-chaos/posts/2016/04/07-panama-papers-putin-gaddy

The Fonseca Fallout

The Panama Papers are starting to have a major impact on the world. We may not feel this here in the United States just yet, turn on the television, and you will hardly hear a word about the Panama Papers from the major news outlets. In Europe and Latin American, however, this is big news and is quite disruptive. We have already seen the Icelandic Prime Minister step down as well as other officials. David Cameron of the U.K is holding on by a thread, and it is not outside of the realm of possibility that he too will have to step aside.

On a much broader level, the Panama Papers have opened up several channels for discussion on Tax havens, financial transparency, limits on the power of sovereign nations and the like. In this chapter, we will discuss the broad implications of the Panama Papers.

The Future of Tax Havens:

It has become apparent that the Tax Havens of the world are going to be under enormous pressure. Nations the world over are slowly blacklisting countries that are considered Tax Havens. This will effectively shut down the industry. No LEGITMATE business will want to do business with a blacklisted country. I think this trend is detrimental. One of the main reasons this trend is gaining traction is because the public has a general misconception about the role tax havens serve. Yes, tax havens are used to evade taxes illegal, but they are also used for tax AVOIDANCE. To most, tax avoidance and tax evasion are the same. If you aren't paying taxes, you are criminal. However, the definitions of avoidance and evasion are starkly different.

Tax avoidance: is a legal way of minimizing taxes; Businesses as well as individuals avoid taxes by taking all legitimate deductions on their tax returns and by sheltering income from taxes by setting up various forms of retirement accounts or corporate structures.

Tax Evasion: Is the illegal practice of not paying taxes, by not reporting income fully, reporting expenses that are not considered legal, or by not paying taxes owed.

Tax havens can facilitate both kinds of transactions; unfortunately, the few that are committing crimes are impacting those who use them for legitimate purposes.

If Tax Havens are abolished, investments abroad will also suffer. For example, let's assume an investor sees an opportunity in Latin America. However, the country in question does not allow direct investment by American Citizens. Their banking laws, however, does not restrict foreign corporations from investing. The American Investor would simply open up a company in the British Virgin islands for example, and through it, can invest in said Latin American country. This is not illegal, is it a roundabout way of doing things? Sure, but it is well within the law. Yes, people also use this to skirt sanctions as well.

We will always have those who will abuse the system. We should not ban an entire industry just because a few break the law. Cars are a wonderful means of transportation. Would we ban the car because a few people have used a car as a weapon? Should we ban credit cards because a few people default on their credit card payments or use credit for illegal purposes? Should we close down fast-food companies because a few people overeat and get sick? No, we would never do this because the benefits outweigh the risks. Tax Havens and offshore entities have been used for decades as a legitimate way to increase investment and decrease unnecessary tax overpayment. Almost every single company in American worth its salt has some connection to offshore entities. http://america.aljazeera.com/articles/2015/10/6/top-us-companies-keep-21-trillion-in-tax-havens-abroad.html

Companies would not need to go offshore if the tax environment in their home countries was favorable to business. It's as simple as that.

On a personal level, we do this all the time. If you can get an item for $100 in one place or for $50 in another, more often than not, you will go to the place offering the same service for $50. It's just common sense. You will give your business to those who give you the better deal. It would be very beneficial if some of the major corporations paid more taxes at home, but they won't so long as the tax system is unfavorable to them. They are by no means breaking the law. In fact, the savings they generate from moving offshore allows for the goods they produce to be cheaper in their own respective home countries.

If Apple, for example, were to pay the top U.S. tax rate for corporations, they would see nearly 40% of their profits gone after deductions. Do you think this would not impact I-Phone prices here at home? It sure would. It's just basic economics, not some evil grand plan to bankrupt America. The United States needs to create incentives for business that are substantial enough to encourage some repatriation of U.S. Dollars aboard. It is easier said than done, that is a certainty. It will be interesting to see how the Financial Landscape will change in response to the Panama Papers. One thing that seems apparent is that the Offshore Industry has sustained a deep wound, one which may prove fatal.

Sovereign Nations and Transparency:

It is hard to determine how many of the transactions revealed in the Panama Papers are illegal. Clearly, some are, but many are not. The majority of the nations exposed do not have laws against offshore ownership, but they do have laws about disclosure. The Prime Minster of Iceland was ousted not because he had offshore holdings, it was because he did not disclose them properly. This lack of transparency is what drove him out. It appears this is the case for David Cameron as well; it was not illegal for him to own shares in an offshore unit trust; it was, however, inappropriate of him to not fully disclose it. Now that he came clean, it hasn't really helped him much. President Obama will be meeting with him in the U.K. on April 22nd, in the hopes of saving Cameron. Obama is very popular in the U.K, with close to a 75% approval rating. Cameron is hoping for some Obama magic. Sadly, that will probably not do much to save him. He may or may not resign, but his lack of initial transparency as well as his other concerns regarding EU membership and his fumbling with the migrant issue may very well drive him out.

As I mentioned earlier in the book, the western nations have been especially hard hit by the Panama Papers and several laws or proposed laws will be discussed regarding financial transparency. Despite the bad press certain EU members have received, it is not in the best interest for all involved to ban offshore investments. France might be on board, Germany as well, but others may not. For example, Cyprus. Luxemburg and Malta may not easily embrace more liberal secrecy laws. This will be a challenge for the E.U. and for all nations for that matter. They will not be able to force every member and country to enact stricter transparency laws; a comprise might have to be reached. And even if a fair-minded agreement can be reached, global cooperation will be uneven at best.

Final Thoughts

Secrecy surrounding financial dealings is nothing new. For ages, we have read accounts of powerful individuals circumventing the system for their own gain, legal or not. So in this sense, the Panama Papers did not reveal anything we did not already know. Is it a surprise that associates of Vladimir Putin may be straw men for Vladimir himself? Is it a surprise that relatives of Bashar Al-Assad own half of Syria's wealth through these shell companies? Is it shocking to find out that drug dealers hide their money on remote islands? No, these are all things we have always known or have suspected on some level. Where there are laws, there will be individual who will break them. Unless tax laws change in ways that don't penalize the rich or the poor, for that matter, these circumventions will continue.

The Panama Papers have truly hit a nerve, not only has it exposed a hidden world of dark money, but it also displays for all to see the vulnerability even the most powerful of people face. We are in a digital age now, and our personal information is under assault. It only takes a few pimply faced 15 year olds in front of a computer to hack into our most sensitive data. Privacy, even for those with deep pockets cannot be guaranteed anymore. To me, that is the broader lesson to be learned from the Panama Papers fiasco. Take Heed...The Hackers are coming.

Recommended Reading

Treasure Islands: Uncovering the Damage of Offshore Banking and Tax Havens Nicholas Shaxson

The Hidden Wealth of Nations: The Scourge of Tax Havens
Gabriel Zucman

The New Confessions of an Economic Hit Man
John Perkins

Narconomics: How to Run a Drug Cartel
Tom Wainwright

Dark Territory: The Secret History of Cyber War
Fred Kaplan

The Hacked World Order: How Nations Fight, Trade, Maneuver, and Manipulate in the Digital Age
Adam Segal

Upcoming Books by the Author

www.simonluria.com

Future Volumes of the Panama Papers

The Self Victimization of A People: How Judaism Fosters Antisemitism

Radical Islam: The Great Satan of the East

Krokodil Tears: The Drug That Could Destroy the World

The False Promise of Reward: How Society Promotes Addiction

Source Material

- "David Cameron urged to act on Panama Papers as UK named 'at heart of super-rich tax-avoidance network'". The Independent. April 5, 2016. Archived from the original on April 4, 2010. Retrieved April 7, 2016.

- "Panama Papers: How Nuix Helped Uncover the Facts". Nuix. Archived from the original on April 8, 2016. Retrieved April 6, 2016.

- Frederik Obermaier; Bastian Obermayer; Vanessa Wormer; Wolfgang Jaschensky. "All you need to know about the Panama Papers". Süddeutsche Zeitung. Retrieved April 5, 2016.

- "Panama Papers Q&A: What is the scandal about?". BBC News. Retrieved 2016-04-07.

- Dearden, Lizzie (April 4, 2016). "Everything you need to know about the Panama Papers". The Independent. Retrieved April 7, 2016.

- Garside, Juliette; Watt, Holly; Pegg, David (April 3, 2016). "The Panama Papers: how the world's rich and famous hide their money offshore". The Guardian. Archived from the original on April 3, 2016. Retrieved April 3, 2016.

- Zoromé, Ahmed (April 1, 2007). "Concept of Offshore Financial Centers: In Search of an Operational Definition" (PDF).

IMF Working Papers. International Monetary Fund. p. 4. Retrieved 2016-04-06.

↑ ↑ "Panama Papers and Mossack Fonseca explained". Australian Broadcasting CORP. April 4, 2016. Retrieved April 4, 2016.

↑ ↑ Salimah Shivji. "Panama Papers: Quebec lawye\Panama Papers: Vladimir Putin associates, Jackie Chan identified in unprecedented leak of offshore financial records"".

↑ ↑ "Places in the sun: a special report on offshore finance" (PDF). The Economist. February 24, 2007. ISSN 0013-0613. Archived from the original on 2007-02-24. Retrieved 2016-04-06.

↑ ↑ Harari, Morgan; Meinzer, Markus; Murphy, Richard (October 1, 2012). "Financial Secrecy, Banks and the Big 4 Firms of Accountants" (PDF). Tax Justice Network. Retrieved 2016-04-06.

↑ ↑ Leyendecker, Hans; Obermaier, Frederik; Obermayer, Bastian; Wormer, Vanessa. "Panama Papers: The Firm". Süddeutsche Zeitung. Retrieved April 7, 2016.

↑ ↑ Harding, Luke (April 3, 2016). "The Panama Papers: what you need to know". The Guardian. ISSN 0261-3077. Archived from the original on April 3, 2016. Retrieved 4 April 2016.

↑ ↑ The Panama Papers and Tax Morality Chohan, Usman W. Academic Discussion Paper, UNSW Canberra and Social Science Research Network [SSRN] (2016)

↑ ↑ "Panama Papers: Vladimir Putin associates, Jackie Chan identified in unprecedented leak of offshore financial records".

ABC News online. 4 April 2016. Retrieved 18 April. Check date values in: |access-date= (help)

↑ ↑ Patricia Cohen (19 January 2016). "Wealth inequality rising fast, Oxfam says, faulting tax havens". Boston Globe. Retrieved 17 April 2016.

↑ ↑ Butagira, Tabu. "Leaked emails expose Heritage plot to dodge Uganda tax". ANCIR.

↑ ↑ Lashmar, Paul (April 3, 2016). "Panama Papers: remarkable global media operation holds rich and powerful to account". The Conversation. Retrieved April 7, 2016.

↑ ↑ "Panama: Report on Observance of Standards and Codes—FATF Recommendations for Anti-Money Laundering and Combating the Financing of Terrorism" (PDF) (PDF). International Monetary Fund.

↑ ↑ "Panama: the making of a tax haven and rogue state". tax justice network.

↑ ↑ "2013 Investment Climate Statement – Panama". U.S. State Department.

↑ ↑ "Panama and OECD: Sanctionatory measures against Panama expected from October 2015". taxinsights.ey.com.

↑ ↑ "Panama Papers: Tax avoidance issue to be taken up at G20 Leaders' Summit". Indian Express. 14 April 2016. Retrieved 18 April 2016.

⯑ ⯑ Anne Michel; Maxime Vaudano (16 April 2016). "" Panama papers " : Panama, Vanuatu et Liban sont menacés de figurer sur la liste noire des paradis fiscaux". Le Monde. Retrieved 18 April 2016.

⯑ ⯑ Vasilyeva, Natalya; Anderson, Mae (April 3, 2016). "News Group Claims Huge Trove of Data on Offshore Accounts". The New York Times. Associated Press. Retrieved April 4, 2016.

⯑ ⯑ Obermaier, Frederik; Obermayer, Bastian; Wormer, Vanessa; Jaschensky, Wolfgang (April 3, 2016). "About the Panama Papers". Süddeutsche Zeitung. Archived from the original on April 3, 2016. Retrieved April 3, 2016.

⯑ ⯑ "Giant leak of offshore financial records exposes global array of crime and corruption". OCCRP. The International Consortium of Investigative Journalists. April 3, 2016. Archived from the original on April 3, 2016.

⯑ ⯑ Greenberg, Andy (April 4, 2016). "How Reporters Pulled Off the Panama Papers, the Biggest Leak in Whistleblower History". Wired. Condé Nast. Retrieved April 4, 2016.

⯑ ⯑ "Panama Papers: Why 'John Doe' risked their life for the Mossack Fonseca leak". Australian Broadcasting Commission. April 5, 2016. Retrieved April 5, 2016.

⯑ ⯑ Kraft, Steffen (August 25, 2011). "Leck bei Wikileaks" [Leak at Wikileaks]. Der Freitag (in German). Archived from the original on March 7, 2012. Retrieved March 7, 2012.

"DocumentCloud 149 Results Source: Internal documents from Mossack Fonseca (Panama) – Provider: Amazon Technologies / Owner: Perfect Privacy, LLC".

Zeitung, Süddeutsche. "All you need to know about the Panama Papers". Süddeutsche.de. Retrieved April 5, 2016.

"From Encrypted Drives To Amazon's Cloud – The Amazing Flight of the Panama Papers". Forbes.

Andy Calloway. "Did an Out of Date WordPress Plugin Expose Mossack Fonseca to Hacks?".

"Slider Revolution Plugin Critical Vulnerability Being Exploited". Sucuri Blog.

Bilton, Richard (April 3, 2016). "Panama Papers: Mossack Fonseca leak reveals elite's tax havens". BBC News. Archived from the original on April 3, 2016. Retrieved April 3, 2016.

Snowden, Edward. "Biggest leak in the history of data journalism just went live, and it's about corruption". Twitter. Archived from the original on April 3, 2016. Retrieved April 3, 2016.

White, Micah (April 5, 2016). "The Panama Papers: leaktivism's coming of age". The Guardian. Comment is Free. Retrieved April 6, 2016.

"Panama Papers: WikiLeaks calls for data leak to be released in full". The Belfast Telegraph. April 5, 2016.

- "Panama Papers: The Power Players". International Consortium of Investigative Journalists. Archived from the original on April 3, 2016. Retrieved April 3, 2016.

- Fusion Investigative Unit (April 3, 2016). "Here are the famous politicos in 'the Wikileaks of the mega-rich'". Fusion. Archived from the original on April 3, 2016. Retrieved April 3, 2016.

- "Rise.md: #PanamaPapers. Conexiunile offshore ale lui Ion Sturza. Proiectul de investigatie globala il are in vizor si pe fostul premier". Moldova: Pro TV Chișinău. April 4, 2016.

- "Giant Leak of Offshore Financial Records Exposes Global Array of Crime and Corruption". Panama Papers (International Consortium of Investigative Journalists). April 3, 2016.

- "The Power Players: Clive Khulubuse Zuma". ICIJ. Retrieved April 3, 2016.

- "Panama Papers: Sarah Ferguson, Simon Cowell and Heather Mills among celebrities named in leak". ProTV. Retrieved April 7, 2016.

- Gibson, Owen (April 3, 2016). "Leaked papers give Fifa ethics committee new credibility crisis". The Guardian. Archived from the original on April 3, 2016. Retrieved April 3, 2016.

- "Group of death: FIFA officials' financial secrets exposed in new Wikileaks-style trove". Fusion. April 3, 2016. Retrieved April 3, 2016.

- BBC Sports. ["Panama Papers: Uefa offices searched by Swiss police"](). BBC.

- Hall, Kevin G.; Taylor, Marisa (April 4, 2016). ["Americans, including a Bellevue man, show up in Panama Papers"](). Seattle Times. Retrieved April 5, 2016.

- ["Panama Papers: The Elites' Shield From Laws Imposed On Us"](). Investor's Business Daily (Los Angeles). April 4, 2016. Retrieved April 6, 2016.

- Christopher Harder (5 April 2016). ["Panama Leak Involves Firm Probed in Petrobras Scandal — Energy Journal"](). Wall Street Journal. Retrieved 18 April 2016.

- Cox, Simon (April 4, 2016). ["Panama Papers: Mossack Fonseca 'helped firms subject to sanctions'"](). BBC. Retrieved April 6, 2016.

- US Department of the Treasury (June 27, 2013). ["Treasury Sanctions Bank, Front Company, and Official Linked to North Korean Weapons of Mass Destruction Programs:Action Targets North Korea's Use of Deceptive Financial Practices to Support its Weapons Programs"](). Retrieved April 6, 2016.

- Garside, Juliette; Harding, Luke (April 4, 2016). ["British banker set up firm 'used by North Korea to sell weapons'"](). The Guardian. ISSN [0261-3077](). Retrieved 2016-04-05.

- ["The Power Players: Mamadou Pouye"](). ICIJ.

- ["Saudi King, UAE President at the Center of the Panama Papers"](). TeleSUR. April 4, 2016.

- "The Panama Papers: Pages from Pakistan". Center for Investigative Reporting in Pakistan (CIRP). April 4, 2016. Retrieved April 5, 2016.

- "Jackie Chan, involucrado en escándalo "Panama Papers"". April 4, 2016. Retrieved April 4, 2016.

- Danielle Wiener-Bronner; David Matthews; Fusion Investigative Unit (6 April 2016). "Here are the most famous celebrities with ties to the huge Panama Papers leak". Retrieved 17 April 2016.

- Ferro, Shane (April 3, 2016). "Icelandic Prime Minister Had Stake in Failed Banks, Leaks Suggest". The Huffington Post. Retrieved April 4, 2016.

- "Iceland's PM says he will not resign in Panama Papers scandal". Belfast Telegraph. April 4, 2016. Retrieved April 4, 2016. He allegedly sold his half of the company to Palsdottir for one US dollar on 31 December 31, 2009, the day before a new Icelandic law took effect that would have required him to declare the ownership of Wintris as a conflict of interest.

- Bowers, Simon (April 3, 2016). "Iceland's PM faces calls for snap election after offshore revelations". The Guardian. Archived from the original on April 3, 2016. Retrieved April 3, 2016.

- Edward Snowden [Snowden] (April 4, 2016). "The population of Iceland is only 330,000. Largest protest by percentage of population in history? #PanamaPapers" (Tweet).

- "Panama Papers leak leads to 'largest protest' in Iceland's history". RT International. April 5, 2016. Retrieved April 5, 2016.

- McKernan, Bethan (April 5, 2016). "People in Iceland are throwing yoghurt at parliament over the Panama Papers". indy100. Retrieved April 5, 2016.

- "Iceland PM: "I will not resign"". Iceland Monitor (Morgunblaðið). April 4, 2016. Retrieved April 4, 2016.

- "Iceland's President refuses PM's request to dissolve parliament amid Panama Papers controversy". The Independent. April 5, 2016. Retrieved April 5, 2016.

- "Panama Papers fallout: Iceland's prime minister resigns". CNN. April 5, 2016. Retrieved April 5, 2016.

- "Prime Minister has not resigned – sends press release to international media". Iceland Monitor. Retrieved April 6, 2016.

- Rayner, Gordon; Morgan, Tom; Riley-Smith, Ben; McCann, Kate (April 6, 2016). "Panama Papers: offshore firm set up by Cameron's father was moved to Ireland in year son became PM". The Telegraph. Retrieved April 6, 2016.

- "Leaked documents show the Mexican president's close friend moved $100 million offshore after a corruption probe". Business Insider. April 5, 2016.

- Simon Bowers. "How Mossack Fonseca helped hide millions from Britain's biggest gold bullion robbery". the Guardian. Retrieved April 5, 2016.

- "The Panama Papers Numbers". panamapapers.icij.org. Retrieved April 4, 2016.

- "US scolds others about offshores, but looks other way at home". Kansas City Star. April 5, 2016. Retrieved April 6, 2016.

- Irving Delgado Nay (April 4, 2016). "MP investigará a Mossack Fonseca" [MP investigated Mossack Fonseca]. El Siglo (in Spanish). Retrieved April 5, 2016.

- "Credit Suisse, HSBC dismiss 'Panama Papers' tax avoidance allegations". United Kingdom: Reuters. April 5, 2016. Retrieved April 5, 2016.

- Kjell Lindroos (April 4, 2016). "Nordea grundade hundratals skatteparadisbolag åt kunder | Svenska Yle" [Nordea founded hundreds of tax haven companies on behalf of customers] (in Swedish).

- "Monday's papers". YLE. April 4, 2016. Retrieved April 4, 2016.

- "svd Detta behöver du veta om Panamaläckan" [Everything you need to know about the Panama Papers leak] (in Swedish). April 4, 2016.

- "Nordea bank investigated over tax haven scandal". The Local (Sweden). Retrieved April 4, 2016.

- "gp Löfven: Nordea på skämslistan" (in Swedish). April 4, 2016.[dead link]

- "Finansministern om Nordea: "Helt oacceptabelt"" (in Swedish). Svenska Dagbladet. April 4, 2016. Archived from the original on April 9, 2016. Retrieved April 6, 2016.

- Miami Herald staff (April 3, 2016). "Mossack Fonseca responds to Miami Herald 'Secret Shell Game' series on offshore companies". The Miami Herald. Retrieved April 3, 2016.

- "The Panama Papers: 7 things to know". CNN. April 5, 2016. Retrieved April 5, 2016.

- "Panama-Papers: Kanzlei Mossack Fonesca erstattet Anzeige" [Panama-papers: Law firm of Mossack Fonesca charges]. DiePresse.com (in German). April 6, 2016. Retrieved 2016-04-08.

- "Statement Regarding Recent Media Coverage" (PDF) (PDF). Mossack Fonseca. Archived from the original (PDF) on April 6, 2016. Retrieved 2016-04-08.

- Blake Schmidt (April 4, 2016). "A Conversation With Panama's Suddenly Notorious Offshore Lawyers". Bloomberg.

- "Panama Papers: Leak firm Mossack Fonseca 'victim of hack'". BBC News. April 6, 2016. Retrieved April 7, 2016.

- "The Latest: Venezuela to Probe Citizens in 'Panama Papers'". The New York Times. Retrieved April 7, 2016.

- León, Guadalupe (April 7, 2016). "Jürgen Mossack renunció al Consejo Nacional de Relaciones Exteriores". La Estrella de Panamá. La Estrella de Panamá. Retrieved April 7, 2016.

- "Vicepresidente y Canciller Varela se reúne con el Consejo Nacional de Relaciones Exteriores" [Vice President and Chancellor Varela meets with the National Foreign Affairs Council] (in Spanish). Retrieved April 7, 2016.

- "DEPARTAMENTO CONSULAR DE LA DGPE MINISTERIO DE RELACIONES EXTERIORES GUIA CONSULAR (actualizada al 6 de abril 2016)" (PDF). MINISTERIO DE RELACIONES EXTERIORES (in Spanish). MINISTERIO DE RELACIONES EXTERIORES PANAMA. Retrieved April 7, 2016.

- "DEPARTAMENTO CONSULAR DE LA DGPE MINISTERIO DE RELACIONES EXTERIORES GUIA CONSULAR (AGOSTO 2013)" (PDF). MINISTERIO DE RELACIONES EXTERIORES (in Spanish). MINISTERIO DE RELACIONES EXTERIORES PANAMA. Retrieved April 7, 2016.

- "DEPARTAMENTO CONSULAR DE LA DGPE MINISTERIO DE RELACIONES EXTERIORES GUIA CONSULAR (Febrero 2011)" (PDF). MINISTERIO DE RELACIONES EXTERIORES (in Spanish). MINISTERIO DE RELACIONES EXTERIORES PANAMA. Retrieved April 7, 2016.

- "DEPARTAMENTO CONSULAR DE LA DGPE MINISTERIO DE RELACIONES EXTERIORES GUIA CONSULAR (Oct 2010)" (PDF). MINISTERIO DE RELACIONES EXTERIORES (in Spanish). MINISTERIO DE RELACIONES EXTERIORES PANAMA. Retrieved April 8, 2016.

- "MP investigará a Mossack Fonseca& – El Siglo". April 4, 2016. Retrieved April 5, 2016.

- "Panamá se defiende y califica de 'irrespetuosas' declaraciones de la OCDE". April 5, 2016. Retrieved April 5, 2016.

- "Panamá se defiende y califica de 'irrespetuosas' declaraciones de la OCDE". April 5, 2016. Retrieved April 6, 2016.

- "Eduardo Morgan: "detrás de todo esto está la OCDE"". April 5, 2016. Retrieved April 6, 2016.

- "'Panama Papers', una campaña de difamación al país: Adolfo Linares". April 5, 2016. Retrieved April 6, 2016.

- "Gremio de abogados insta a Gobierno panameño demandar por daño de imagen". April 6, 2016. Retrieved April 7, 2016.

- "Panamá sale afectado". April 5, 2016. Retrieved April 7, 2016.

- "Repercución económica". April 5, 2016. Retrieved April 7, 2016.

- "Repudian ataque a imagen del país". April 6, 2016. Retrieved April 7, 2016.

- "Sociedades offshore". April 5, 2016. Retrieved April 7, 2016.

- "Fiscalía panameña realizó allanamiento en Mossack Fonseca". April 12, 2016. Retrieved April 13, 2016.

- "Macri, imputado por las cuentas offshore" [Macri, charged with offshore accounts] (in Spanish). Pagina 12. April 7, 2016. Retrieved 2016-04-07.

- "Panamá Papers: imputaron a Mauricio Macri por su participación en una sociedad offshore" [Papers Panama: Mauricio Macri charged to its participation in an offshore company].

www.lanacion.com.ar (in Spanish). April 7, 2016. Retrieved 2016-04-07.

▫ ▫ "Macri fue director de una sociedad offshore de Bahamas" [Macri was director of an offshore company in the Bahamas]. www.lanacion.com.ar (in Spanish). Retrieved 2016-04-07.

▫ ▫ "Macri offshore: aparece una segunda empresa del presidente en Panamá - Perfil.com" [Macri offshore: appears a second company president in Panama]. Perfil.com (in Spanish). Retrieved 2016-04-07.

▫ ▫ "Big names implicated in Panama Papers offshore banking leak: Lionel Messi, Jackie Chan, several current and former world leaders among names revealed". CBC News. 4 April 2016. Retrieved 18 April 2016.

▫ ▫ "Los Messi dicen que nunca usaron la sociedad panameña" [Meshttp://www.abc.net.au/news/2016-04-04/fifa-officials-and-lionel-messi-named-in-offshore-files/7296140si say they never used the Panamanian society] (in Spanish). April 4, 2016. Retrieved April 4, 2016.

▫ ▫ Australian Broadcast Corp (3 April 2016). "Panama Papers: FIFA officials, Lionel Messi, Michel Platini named in secret offshore files". Retrieved 18 April 2016.

▫ ▫ Associated Press (8 October 2015). "Lionel Messi to face tax fraud charges: Judge rejects request to clear Barcelona player". CBC Sport. Retrieved 18 April 2016.

- "Mihran Poghosyan: The Armenian General Who Mastered the Ins and Outs of Panama's Offshore Zone". Hetq Online. April 4, 2016. Retrieved April 11, 2016.

- "The General: An Armenian Master of Offshores". OCCRP. April 8, 2016. Retrieved April 11, 2016.

- "Panama Papers Fallout in Armenia; Local NGO Files Petition to Launch Investigation of Top Official". Hetq Online. April 8, 2016. Retrieved April 11, 2016.

- Chenoweth, Neil (April 4, 2016). "Panama Papers: ATO investigating more than 800 Australian clients of Mossack Fonseca". Sydney Morning Herald. Retrieved April 4, 2016.

- "Offshore companies provide link between corporate mogul and Azerbaijan's president". ICIJ. April 3, 2016. Retrieved April 11, 2016.

- "Bangladeshis not outside Panama Papers". www.observerbd.com. The Daily Observer. Retrieved April 7, 2016.

- Law Firm At Center of Panama Papers Leak Was Implicated In Brazil Corruption Scandal In January by Keren Blankfeld ,F in Forbes (2016)

- Brazil politicians linked to offshore companies in Panama leaks: paper by Silvio Cascione "Reuters" (2016)

- Brazilian Media Giant Globo Implicated in the Panama Papers by teleSUR (2016)

⁃ ⁃ [Joaquim Barbosa é o primeiro destaque brasileiro no escândalo da Mossack Fonseca.](#) by Paulo Nogueira in "Diario do Centro do Mundo" newspaper (2016) (Portuguese)

⁃ ⁃ ["Brazil's former top judge hid price he paid for Miami condo"](#). [Miami Herald](#). 3 April 2016. Retrieved 5 April 2016.

⁃ ⁃ [A guide to the 5 biggest revelations from the Panama Papers (so far)](#) por Tara Golshan na "Vox Media" (2016) (Portuguese)

⁃ ⁃ Fife, Robert (April 7, 2016). "Trudeau says he does not have money in offshore accounts". The Globe and Mail. The Globe and Mail Inc.

⁃ ⁃ ["CRA seeks Panama Papers to search for new clues about tax cheats"](#). CBC News. 5 April 2016. Retrieved 18 April 2016.

⁃ ⁃ ["RBC denies wrongdoing after being named in Panama Papers: 'There are a number of legitimate reasons' to set up foreign holding companies, bank spokesman says"](#). CBC News. 4 April 2016. Retrieved 18 April 2016.

⁃ ⁃ ["Royal Bank and BMO defend Canada's banking sector amid Panama Papers and Fintrac fine"](#). CBC News. CBC/Radio-Canada. April 7, 2016. Retrieved April 9, 2016. Canadian banks have "dramatically" beefed up anti-money laundering controls over the last seven to 10 years

⁃ ⁃ Scuffham, Matt (April 6, 2016). ["Royal Bank of Canada sets up team to scrutinize data exposed in Panama Papers leak"](#). Financial Post. O Canada. Retrieved April 9, 2016.

- Schmitz, Rob (April 4, 2016). "Xi Jinping's family linked to Panama Papers". Marketplace. Retrieved April 6, 2016.

- "Panama papers: China censors online discussion". BBC News. Retrieved April 5, 2016.

- Kaiman, Jonathan (April 5, 2016). "China censors media coverage about the 'Panama Papers'". Los Angeles Times. Retrieved April 5, 2016.

- "【真理部】自查自删涉"巴拿马文件"泄露事件所有相关内容" ["Ministry of Truth" changed the truth by deleting all "Panama file" related content] (in Chinese). China Digital Times. Retrieved April 8, 2016.

- "【敏感词库】"Panama"、冰岛总理辞职等热点 2016-4-05". China Digital Times. China Digital Times. Retrieved April 8, 2016.

- Caide, Fu; Shuangzhou, Wang (April 6, 2016). "权贵家族上榜，中国封锁"巴拿马文件"相关报道" [China blocked "Panama files"; family of dignitaries listed] (in Chinese) (The New York Times). The New York Times. Retrieved April 8, 2016.

- Casa Editorial El Tiempo (April 4, 2016). "Colombianos que aparecen en lista de Papeles de Panamá – Sectores – ELTIEMPO.COM". El Tiempo.

- "Lista de paraísos fiscales para Colombia" [List of tax havens for Colombia], Legis Comunidad Contable, October 23, 2014, retrieved April 5, 2016

- "Colombia and Panama to hold new talks on tax info sharing", Reuters, April 12, 2016, retrieved April 13, 2016

- Angelos Anastasiou (April 4, 2016)Cyprus implicated in Panama papers, Cyprus Mail, retrieved April 5, 2016.

- Quentin, Ariès; Paravinci, Giulia (April 7, 2016). "5 ways the Panama Papers swept up EU figures". POLITICO. Retrieved April 7, 2016.

- Ariès, Quentin (April 6, 2016). "EU vows to act quickly on Panama Papers". POLITICO. Retrieved April 7, 2016.

- Stewart, Heather (April 6, 2016). "Cameron stepped in to shield offshore trusts from EU tax crackdown in 2013". The Guardian. Retrieved April 7, 2016.

- "Panama Papers: Cameron's 2013 concern over trust reforms". BBC News. April 7, 2016. Retrieved April 7, 2016.

- "Will Britain Leave The EU Over The Panama Papers? How David Cameron May Affect The Brexit Vote". International Business Times. April 4, 2016. Retrieved April 7, 2016.

- France opens probe after Panama leaks, Reuters (April 4, 2016).

- "Francia vuelve a poner a Panamá en su lista de refugios fiscales" (in Spanish). April 5, 2016. Retrieved April 5, 2016.

- Agence France-Presse (19 March 2013). "Jérôme Cahuzac démissionne". Retrieved 18 April 2016.

- Angelique Chrisafis (2 April 2013). "France's former budget minister admits lying about secret offshore account". Retrieved 18 April 2016.

- "Le bureau national du PS exclut Jérôme Cahuzac à l'unanimité". Le Monde. 9 April 2003. Retrieved 18 April 2016.

- Simon Piel (20 April 2015). "Premier bilan mitigé pour le parquet financier". Le Monde. Retrieved 18 April 2016.

- "L'affaire Riwal, le Bygmalion version FN". L'Expresse. 1 March 2015. Retrieved 18 April 2016.

- "Enquête du parquet financier sur le patrimoine de Marine Le Pen". Reuters France. 7 January 2016. Retrieved 18 April 2016.

- Marc de Boni (3 October 2015). "Quand les partis rémunèrent leurs cadres avec l'argent de Bruxelles". Le Figaro. Retrieved 18 April 2016.

- "City Councilperson Resigns". The Reykjavík Grapevine. Retrieved April 5, 2016.

- Sarin, Ritu; Iyer, P Vaidyanathan; Mazoomdaar, Jay (April 4, 2016). "Indians in Panama Papers list: Amitabh Bachchan,

Aishwarya Rai, KP Singh, Iqbal Mirchi, Adani elder brother". The Indian Express. Retrieved April 5, 2016.

▢ ▢ Manu Balachandran. "From Bollywood stars to real estate tycoons: the Indians in Panama Papers". www.msn.com. Quartz.

▢ ▢ "PM Modi steps in: Income Tax, RBI panel to probe Panama Papers trail". The Indian Express. April 4, 2016.

▢ ▢ "Menkeu Tugaskan Dirjen Pajak Telusuri Temuan Panama Papers". CNN Indonesia. April 5, 2016.

▢ ▢ "Israel to Probe Hundreds Implicated by Panama Papers". Haaretz.com. Retrieved April 5, 2016.

▢ ▢ "600 Israeli companies, 850 shareholders listed in Panama data leak". The Times of Israel. Retrieved April 5, 2016.

▢ ▢ di ROBERTO PETRINI (April 6, 2016). "Panama Papers, procure italiane al lavoro. La Guardia di Finanza indaga per riciclaggio". Repubblica.it.

▢ ▢ "Panama Papers, altri 100 nomi: spuntano Galliani, Barilla, Pessina, Berlusconi e Briatore. E Verdone si difende: "Sono onesto, datemi fiducia"". LaStampa.it. April 14, 2016.

▢ ▢ "Il secondo elenco – Panama Papers, altri 100 nomi: spuntano Galliani, Barilla, Berlusconi e Briatore".

▢ ▢ "We will not allow anyone to tarnish this government with corruption – Joseph Muscat – The Malta Independent".

- "Marlene Farrugia will support no-confidence vote against Mizzi". MaltaToday.com.mt.

- "Keith Schembri denies 'all allegations' made against him; blogger says he is 'lying brazenly' – The Malta Independent".

- "Gaffarena court case: PM rules himself out of being a defendant – The Malta Independent".

- "PN labels Konrad Mizzi, Keith Schembri scandal as 'biggest in Maltese political history' – The Malta Independent".

- Allied Newspapers Ltd. "Updated – Opposition describes situation as 'surreal' as Konrad Mizzi makes statement in parliament, about cemeteries". Times of Malta.

- "A well-connected Mexican tycoon stashes a fortune overseas". The McClatchy DC. April 3, 2016.

- AN, Redaccion (April 4, 2016). "Aún pueden pagar impuestos los mexicanos involucrados en Panama Papers: SAT". Aristegui Noticias. Retrieved April 4, 2016.

- "Mexican Government Contractor Who Built First Lady's Mansion Is Exposed In The Panama Papers". April 4, 2016.

- Wardell, Jane; Moreno, Elida (April 4, 2016). "Tax authorities begin probes into some people named in Panama Papers leak". Reuters. Retrieved April 4, 2016.

- "NZ a 'nice front' for criminals". April 8, 2016. Retrieved April 10, 2016.

- Linn Johansen. "Skatteetaten jakter på 30 nordmenn" [The tax agency hunts of 30 Norwegians]. VG (in Norwegian). Retrieved April 5, 2016.

- Mina Ghabel Lunde. "Fantastisk å være en brikke i et stort grensesprengende prosjekt" [Wonderful to be a cog in a large pioneering project]. www.dn.no (in Norwegian). Retrieved April 5, 2016.

- "Panama Papers: List of Pakistani politicians, businessmen who own companies abroad". Pakistan Today. 4 April 2016. Retrieved 17 April 2016.

- Cheema, Uma (April 4, 2016). "The Panama Papers: Pages From Pakistan". Retrieved April 6, 2016.

- "I do not own any company or property abroad: Maryam Nawaz". Samaa TV. April 4, 2016. Retrieved April 5, 2016.

- "Imran demands immediate probe in Sharif family's alleged offshore wealth". 4 April 2016. Retrieved 18 April 2016.

- "Nawaz's son owns London apartment, offshore companies". Express Tribune. 6 April 2006. Retrieved 18 April 2016.

- Irfan Ghauri (15 April 2016). "All Pakistanis named in Panama Papers face probe". Retrieved 18 April 2016.

- Jay Mazoomdaar (5 April 2016). "In oil-for-food shadow, Benazir Bhutto set up a firm too". Indian Express. Retrieved 17 April 2016.

* Ali Zain (4 April 2016). "Panama Papers: Benazir Bhutto's oil firm paid huge bribes to Iraqi President Saddam Hussain for contracts". Daily Pakistan. Retrieved 17 April 2016.

* http://www.khaleejtimes.com (2 April 2006). "Court orders confiscation of Zardari's entire property". Retrieved 17 April 2016.

* "Panama Papers: Leaks Reveal Abbas' Son's $1m Holding in Company With Ties to Palestinian Authority". Haaretz.com.

* "Panama Papers – All articles by Süddeutsche Zeitung". Panama Papers.

* Harding, Luke (April 3, 2016). "Revealed: the $2bn offshore trail that leads to Vladimir Putin". The Guardian (London).

* "Panama Papers: Putin associates linked to 'money laundering'". BBC News. April 3, 2016. Retrieved April 7, 2016.

* "Золото партитуры" [Gold of the score]. Novaya Gazeta (in Russian) (Moscow). April 3, 2016. Retrieved April 6, 2016. Gold sheet music – Why Sergei Roldugin, a close friend of Vladimir Putin, may be deemed to be not only a virtuoso musician, but also the owner of shady offshore Empire with assets in the billions of dollars

* Harding, Luke (April 4, 2016). "Kremlin dismisses revelations in Panama Papers as 'Putinphobia'". The Guardian. Retrieved April 6, 2016.

* Kim Hjelmgaard; Anna Arutunyan. "Russia says Putin is main target of Panama Papers". USA TODAY.

- Lizzie Dearden. "Vladimir Putin's spokesperson blames 'Putinophobia' for Panama leak". The Independent.

- Howard Amos. "Kremlin Blasts Panama Papers As Putinophobic 'Attack' On Russia Orchestrated By CIA". International Business Times.

- "Panama Papers: Putin rejects corruption allegations". BBC News. April 7, 2016. Retrieved April 7, 2016.

- world_reporter, Jake Rudnitsky Rudnit Ilya Arkhipov. "Putin Sees U.S., Goldman Sachs Behind Leak of Panama Papers". Bloomberg.com. Retrieved 2016-04-15.

- Corcoran, Jason. "Russia Hires Goldman as Corporate Broker to Boost Image". Bloomberg.com. Retrieved 2016-04-15.

- "Kremlin Apologizes for Putin's Goldman Sachs Gaffe". NBC News. Retrieved 2016-04-15.

- "Russian State Media Mostly Ignore Panama Papers". Billboard.

- Tom Balmforth. "The Panama Papers in Russia". The Atlantic.

- "Saudi King, UAE President at the Center of the Panama Papers". TeleSUR. April 4, 2016.

- "A world tour of the politicians named in the Panama Papers". France 24. April 5, 2016.

- "Panama Papers: Singapore reviewing information, doing 'necessary checks'". Channel NewsAsia. Retrieved April 7, 2016.

- "Minister Soria is on the Panama Papers" (in Spanish). eldiario.es. April 11, 2016.

- "José Manuel Soria renounces as Minister of Industry" (in Spanish). El Mundo. April 15, 2016.

- "Panama Papers: Spain's Industry Minister José Manuel Soria Resigns Over Links To Offshore Account". International Business Times. April 15, 2016.

- von Koskul, Casper (April 4, 2016). "Nordea: Vi godtar inte skatteflykt" [Nordea: we do not accept tax evasion] (in Swedish). SVT Nyheter. Retrieved April 4, 2016.

- "'Many' Thais implicated in global scandal". Bangkok Post. April 4, 2016. Retrieved April 5, 2016.

- "Tunisie: le ministère public ouvre une enquête sur le Panama Papers". Réalités. April 5, 2016.

- (French) "Panama Papers : Création d'une commission d'enquête parlementaire". Kapitalis. April 8, 2016.

- Crerar, Pippa; Prynn, Jonathan (October 21, 2015). "Revealed: How foreign buyers have bought £100bn of London property in six years". Evening Standard. Retrieved April 6, 2015.

- Karmanau, Yuras (April 4, 2016). "Ukrainian president under fire over Panama Papers". Associated Press. Retrieved April 4, 2016.

- Luke Harding (April 6, 2016). "Ukraine's leader set up secret offshore firm as battle raged with Russia". Guardian. Retrieved April 7, 2016.

- "Panama Papers: Ukraine President Poroshenko denies tax claims". BBC News. April 4, 2016. Retrieved April 7, 2016.

- Oksana Grytsenko (April 7, 2016). "Anything To Hide?: Revelations undercut trust in Poroshenko". Kyiv Post. Retrieved April 7, 2016.

- David Pegg; Helena Bengtsson; Holly Watt (April 5, 2016). "Revealed: the tycoons and world leaders who built secret UK property empires". The Guardian.

- Myhr, Peder (April 4, 2016). "Panama Papers: Canadians, Putin, Icelandic PM linked to massive offshore tax leak". Global News. Retrieved April 7, 2016.

- Adam Lusher (April 5, 2016). "Panama Papers: 12 world leaders linked to offshore dealings – and the full allegations against them". The Independent. Retrieved April 7, 2016.

- "The Power Players: Ian Cameron". ICIJ. Retrieved April 3, 2016.

- Sabin, Lamiat (April 6, 2016). "Tell us your Tax Secrets and Probe Panama Names". The Morning Star. Retrieved April 6, 2016.

- Rayner, Gordon; Morgan, Tom; Riley-Smith, Ben (April 6, 2016). "Panama Papers: offshore firm set up by Cameron's father was moved to Ireland in year son became PM". The Daily Telegraph. Retrieved April 6, 2016.

↑ ↑ Garside, Juliette (April 4, 2016). "Fund run by David Cameron's father avoided paying tax in Britain". The Guardian. Retrieved April 6, 2016.

↑ ↑ Booth, Robert; Watt, Holly; Pegg, David (April 7, 2016). "David Cameron admits he profited from father's Panama offshore trust fund". The Guardian.

↑ ↑ "The Panama Papers: how the world's rich and famous hide their money offshore". The Guardian. April 3, 2016. Retrieved April 7, 2016.

↑ ↑ "Tory donors' links to offshore firms revealed in leaked Panama Papers". The Guardian. April 4, 2016. Retrieved April 7, 2016.

↑ ↑ Abbott, Diane (April 4, 2015). "Panama Is Just the Tip of the Iceberg: Global Tax Avoidance Is Literally Killing the Poor". The Huffington Post UK. Archived from the original on April 5, 2016. Retrieved April 5, 2016.

↑ ↑ Sabin, Lamiat (April 5, 2016). "Abbott: This Is Just Tip Of The Iceberg". The Morning Star. Archived from the original on April 5, 2016. Retrieved April 5, 2016.

↑ ↑ John McDonnell [johnmcdonnellMP] (April 3, 2016). "The Panama papers revelations are extremely serious. HMRC should treat this with utmost priority and urgently launch investigation" (Tweet). Archived from the original on April 5, 2016.

⬚ ⬚ Eleftheriou-Smith, Loulla-Mae (April 5, 2016). "Jeremy Corbyn calls for investigation into David Cameron's family over Panama papers link". The Independent. Retrieved April 5, 2016.

⬚ ⬚ "Panama Papers: Corbyn urges action on tax avoidance". BBC News. April 5, 2016. Retrieved April 5, 2016.

⬚ ⬚ "Panama Papers: Jeremy Corbyn calls for investigation into David Cameron's family tax affairs as Tory ex-Attorney General tells PM to come clean". The Daily Telegraph. April 5, 2016. Retrieved April 5, 2016.

⬚ ⬚ Simons, Ned (April 5, 2016). "Panama Papers Revelations Mean David Cameron Must Stop 'Pussyfooting' Around on Tax Dodging, Says Jeremy Corbyn". The Huffington Post UK. Retrieved April 5, 2016.

⬚ ⬚ Norman Baker (April 8, 2016). Tories need to be investigated properly over Panama leak (YouTube video). RT UK.

⬚ ⬚ Nicola Sturgeon (April 8, 2016). Sturgeon calls for "utter transparency from Cameron" (YouTube video). RT UK.

⬚ ⬚ Sparrow, Andrew (April 8, 2016). "Panama Papers hit David Cameron's approval ratings – politics live". The Guardian. Retrieved April 8, 2016.

⬚ ⬚ "'Cameron shouldn't just resign... he should be sent to prison!' Ken Livingstone tells RT". RT International. April 8, 2016.

Archived from the original on April 18, 2016. Retrieved April 8, 2016.

↑ ↑ Alex Salmond (April 8, 2016). 'Cameron not a goner yet' Alex Salmond (YouTube video). RT UK.

↑ ↑ MacDonald, Alistair; Gross, Jenny (April 6, 2016). "'Panama Papers' Raise Pressure on U.K. to Rein in Offshore Tax Havens". Wall Street Journal. Retrieved April 6, 2016.

↑ ↑ "The UK is the most important player in tax havens". ethical consumer. Retrieved April 7, 2016.

↑ ↑ "The Most Popular Tax Havens in the Panama Papers". The Statistics Portal. April 5, 2016. Retrieved April 7, 2016.

↑ ↑ "Cam panned over Panama: Pressure mounts on PM after father and billionaire backers were named in tax avoidance scandal". The Sun. April 5, 2016. Retrieved April 7, 2016.

↑ ↑ Grierson, Jamie; Asthana, Anushka; Mason, Rowena; Walker, Peter (April 5, 2016). "David Cameron must come clean on tax, says Jeremy Corbyn". The Guardian. Retrieved April 5, 2016.

↑ ↑ "Panama Papers: Jeremy Corbyn says David Cameron should impose 'direct rule' to end UK tax havens". The Independent. April 5, 2016. Retrieved April 5, 2016.

↑ ↑ "Panama papers: UK tax havens 'should face direct rule'". BBC News. April 5, 2016. Retrieved April 6, 2016.

- Editorial (April 6, 2016). "Judge The PM on His Deeds". The Morning Star. Retrieved April 6, 2016.

- "UK to hold 'anti corruption summit' in 2016". Financial Times. July 28, 2015. Retrieved April 5, 2016.

- "HMRC ready to follow up Panama papers allegations". ITV News. April 4, 2016. Retrieved April 4, 2016.

- "New Troup movements at HMRC". Private Eye. Retrieved April 11, 2016.

- "HMRC chief was partner at law firm that acted for Cameron offshore fund". The Guardian. April 11, 2016. Retrieved April 11, 2016.

- Bilton, Richard (April 4, 2016). "Panama Papers: How a British man, 90, covered for a US millionaire". BBC News. Retrieved 2016-04-04.

- "Panama Papers: Where are the Americans?". BBC News. April 6, 2016. Retrieved April 6, 2016.

- Higgins, Eoin (April 3, 2016). "No US Names in Panama Papers Leak- Why Not?". eoinhiggins.com. Eoin Higgins. Retrieved April 7, 2016.

- "Foreign Account Tax Compliance Act (FATCA)". www.treasury.gov. Retrieved 2016-04-18.

- U.S. Dept. of the Treasury (November 30, 2010). "Tax Information Exchange Agreement" (PDF). Treasury.gov. U.S. Dept. of the Treasury. Retrieved April 18, 2016.

- "Everyone is freaking out about the Panama Papers—but the biggest fallout is yet to come". Mother Jones. April 4, 2016. Retrieved April 7, 2016.

- Jen Mills (April 4, 2016). "Why are there no US people in the Panama papers?". Metro.co.uk.

- Boland-Rudder, Hamish; Holmes, Allan; Chittum, Ryan. "Impact of Panama Papers rockets around the world; U.S. officials react cautiously". Center for Public Integrity. Retrieved April 7, 2016.

- Mindock, Clark (April 4, 2016). "Panama Papers: Obama, Clinton Pushed Trade Deal Amid Warnings It Would Make Money Laundering, Tax Evasion Worse". International Business Times.

- Cassidy, John (2016-04-05). "Panama Papers: Why Aren't There More American Names?". The New Yorker. ISSN 0028-792X. Retrieved 2016-04-18.

- Resources > Faculty > David P. Weber">"Home > Resources > Faculty > David P. Weber". University of Maryland. Retrieved 18 April 2016.

- ABC Color. "Conmebol renovó con mismos dueños de investigada T&T".

- Tripp Mickle, Patricia Kowsmann and Joe Flint (June 7, 2015). "DirecTV, Fox Worked With FIFA Middlemen". WSJ.

CPSIA information can be obtained
at www.ICGtesting.com
Printed in the USA
LVOW01s0250171016
508997LV00013BB/593/P